HOCKEY
LEGENDS

HOCKEY
LEGENDS

JEFF JACOBS

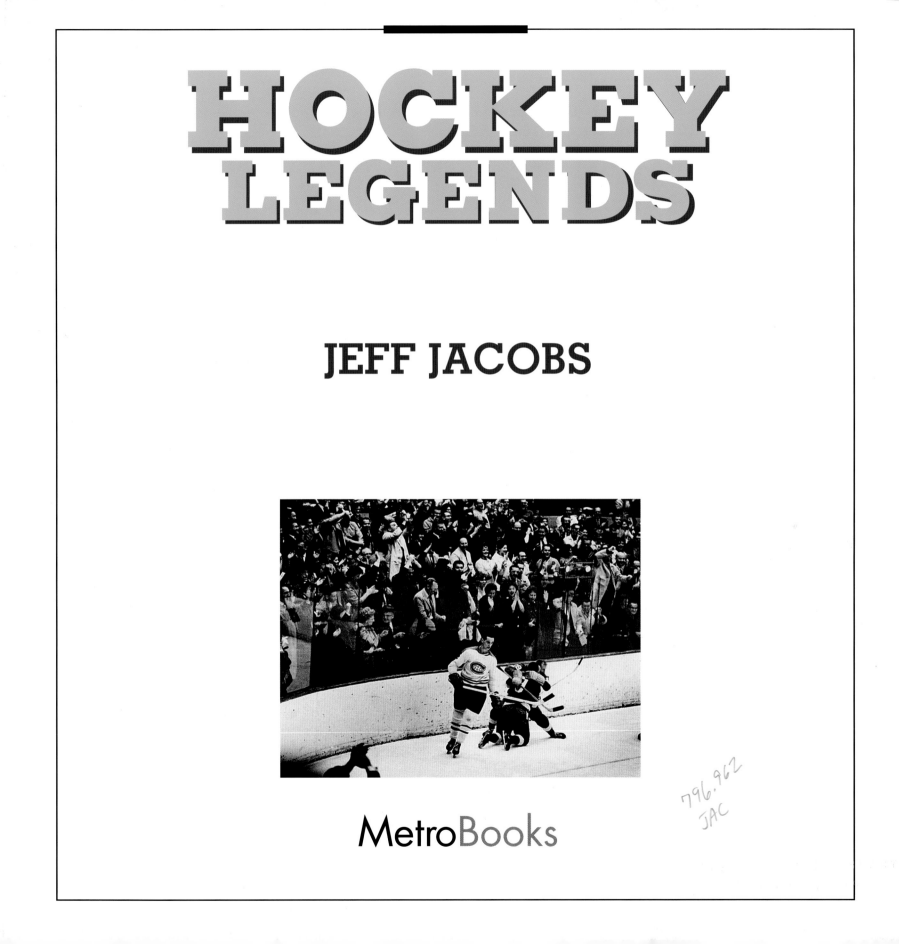

MetroBooks

MetroBooks

An Imprint of Friedman/Fairfax Publishers

© 1995 by Michael Friedman Publishing Group, Inc.

Library of Congress Cataloging-in-Publication Data
    Jacobs, Jeff, date
        Hockey Legends/Jeff Jacobs.
            p. cm.
        Includes biographical references and index.
        ISBN: 1-56799-204-8
        1. Hockey--History. 2. National Hockey League.
        3. Hockey players--Biography. 4. Hockey--Statisics. I. Title.
        GV846.5.J33 1995
        796..962--dc20

                                                95-3328
                                                CIP

Editor: Sharyn Rosart
Art Director: Jeff Batzli
Designer: Joseph Sherman
Photography Editor: Colleen A. Branigan

Color separation by Fine Arts Repro House Co., Ltd.
Printed in China by Leefung-Asco Printers Ltd.

For bulk purchases and special sales, please contact:
Friedman/Fairfax Publishers
Attention: Sales Department
15 West 26th Street
New York, NY 10010
(212) 685-6610 Fax (212) 685-1307

Dedication

For those who love hockey, on both sides of the border and on either side of the Atlantic Ocean.

Acknowledgments

Thanks to those whose patience and expertise made the effort worthwhile: my wife Liz, my daughter Katerina, the National Hockey League, the public relations staff of the Hartford Whalers, my pals in the Professional Hockey Writers Association, editor Sharyn Rosart of the Michael Friedman Publishing Group, and Greg Garber.

14.00

CONTENTS

INTRODUCTION

There is no place in the world of hockey, and perhaps in all of sports, like the Montreal Canadiens' locker room. Peering down from photo-graphs above the locker stalls are the faces of all Les Habitants' Hall of Famers. It's spooky.

Maurice "Rocket" Richard and his brother, Henri, the "Pocket Rocket," are there. And so are Jean Beliveau, Jacques Plante, Howie Morenz, and on and on to Bob Gainey.

All the great ones stare down on the mere mortals who play the game, daring them to be great, challenging them to give their all. There is an inscription in French and English on those walls: "From failing hands we throw the torch; be yours to hold it high." The words are from the poem "In Flanders Fields" penned by soldier John McCrae during World War I.

That war claimed millions of victims, among them great hockey players like "One-Eyed" Frank McGee and Hobey Baker. And some may say that comparing war to sport in any way is in questionable taste. But the torch analogy fits perfectly in this case, for hockey is much more than just a sport, and the Canadiens, with their incredible twenty-four Stanley Cups, are more than just a team. To its fans and players, hockey is a passionate love affair that lasts from one generation to the next. The torch is handed down from parent to child, on and on.

In Canada, hockey is baseball, football, and basketball rolled into one. It is Saturday night in front of the television set for Hockey Night in Canada. It is the grand announcers of the game such as Foster Hewitt and Danny Gallivan. In fact, hockey *is* Canada.

But in New York, Boston, Chicago, and Detroit, the National Hockey League is part of the larger sporting mosaic. And it is growing. In the past, hockey franchises have failed in the Sun Belt, but teams are succeeding now in Florida, Texas, and California.

This success should not come as a surprise, because hockey is a truly great game. It has the collisions and physical fury of football. It has the fast up-and-down pace of basketball. It has the shooter-goalie confrontations of soccer. And when a player like Brett Hull or Al MacInnis rips a slap shot, it is as exciting as when a great home run hitter has just smacked a baseball into the upper deck.

Hockey is the magical playmaking of Wayne Gretzky. Hockey is the flowing blond hair of Guy Lafleur as he races up-ice with the puck. Hockey is the amazing one-on-one moves of Mario Lemieux. Hockey is the great glove save by Grant Fuhr. Hockey is the Montreal Forum and the Boston Garden. Hockey is New York City breaking the Stanley Cup curse of fifty-four years. Hockey is a grand game. And following are its greatest players, finest teams, and most memorable moments.

THE PLAYERS

As part of its seventy-fifth anniversary celebration in 1992, the NHL decided to hold a balloting to name the greatest player at each position in league history. It figured to be highly controversial.

Can you put Wayne Gretzky at center and leave off Jean Beliveau?

How do you differentiate among such brilliant defensemen as Eddie Shore, Bobby Orr, and Doug Harvey?

Gordie Howe's the greatest right-winger of all time, no question. But that leaves Guy Lafleur, Mike Bossy, and Rocket Richard unfairly in the dust.

What to do? The NHL and Pro Set, the sponsor, came up with this solution: the all-time teams would be divided up into three eras. Each would represent a twenty-five-year period. The fans voted for the more recent eras. A special committee selected the winners for the first quarter century.

Although this approach didn't put an end to all the close calls, it certainly took the bite out of many of the controversies.

The truth is that there are about half a dozen dead-cinch all-time stars. Nobody really questions the status of Howe, Orr, Gretzky, or Richard. But there are about thirty players who could legitimately claim legendary status. This chapter describes twenty of them.

Some outstanding players, including Red Kelly, Bryan Trottier, Stan Mikita, and Jacques Plante are not listed among these twenty legends. They should be. Kelly is the only man to master both defense and center positions. Trottier was the best all-around player during the Islanders' dynasty. Mikita was a brilliant centerman for the Blackhawks, conquering all aspects of the game. Plante was the goalie for the 1956–60 championships of the Canadiens, the greatest team ever assembled. I don't feel good about leaving out Ted Lindsay, Paul Coffey, and Frank Mahovlich, either.

But you have to stop somewhere. You could argue about Plante, Terry Sawchuk, and Glenn Hall—goalies of equal stature during the same period—all night long. And if you favor Plante, where does that leave Ken Dryden? Not to mention Grant Fuhr and Patrick Roy, the most recent goaltending greats.

In the end, I based my selection on how those players performed against their peers, their impact on the game at their peak, and whether they demonstrated sustained brilliance. Leadership, crucial plays, and lack of glaring weaknesses also counted.

If you want to add a player of your own to the list of legends, go right ahead.

Opposite: The New York Rangers acquired Mark Messier from Edmonton in October 1991 to bring them an elusive Stanley Cup. In June 1994, Messier delivers. Above: Team captain Wayne Gretzky watched the action as the Kings met the Sabres in March 1993.

JEAN BELIVEAU

Hockey is a game of physical and emotional fire. But Jean Beliveau succeeded as its seeming antithesis. Cool and calm, he played with grace and skill—and the game knew no finer gentleman.

It may be Beliveau's finest testament that nobody in the sport can think of anything bad to say about Le Gros Bill. Unassuming and distinguished, Beliveau played two decades in the NHL and escaped almost all criticism. If Joe DiMaggio had grown up in French Canada and laced up skates instead of picking up a baseball bat, his name would have been Beliveau.

Beliveau's scoring statistics have been surpassed by those who played in the higher tempo and offensive pitch of recent seasons. But when Beliveau retired in 1971, no center ever had scored more than the 1,219 points he amassed. Only Montreal teammate Henri Richard, who added a final championship in 1973, played on more than Beliveau's ten Stanley Cup teams.

Other players dug in hard and pushed to skate. Beliveau, at six feet three inches (190.5cm), seemed to glide effortlessly over the ice with long strides. And except for Wayne Gretzky, there has never been a bettter stickhandler.

Despite all his accomplishments, Beliveau may not have lived up to the enormous expectations that fans had of him. Nobody could have. Few players in NHL history have been more sought-after than Beliveau, who is remembered as much for how he entered the NHL as the way he played in it.

Already a legend as a junior player with the Quebec City Citadels, Beliveau's popularity was the major reason Le Colisée—the arena where the Nordiques play today—was built. Fans flocked to see him play. And rather than move up directly to the Canadiens, he chose to remain in Quebec City to play for the Aces of the Quebec Senior League. Brought up to the Canadiens for three games in 1952–53, Beliveau amassed five goals.

The Canadiens could wait no longer. Beliveau was making a whopping $20,000 in Quebec as an "amateur." In an unprecedented move, the Canadiens bought the entire league, turned it professional, and acquired the players' professional rights. Beliveau got a $20,000 signing bonus and a five-year, $105,000 deal—unheard-of numbers for a rookie in the 1950s. He was worth every nickel of it.

Beliveau played center on arguably the greatest power-play unit ever assembled in the mid-1950s. He won the Hart Trophy twice as the NHL's most valuable player—in a tribute to his longevity, he won it first in 1956 and again in 1964. And when the Conn Smythe Trophy was instituted for the MVP of the playoffs in 1965, Beliveau won that, too.

Maurice Richard (left) and Jean Beliveau (right) hugging the Stanley Cup (here, in 1958) was a pose hockey fans outside Montreal grew to annually despise.

He was named first-team NHL All-Star six times and to the second team four times. Among centers, only Gretzky surpasses these numbers.

Beliveau was the Canadiens' captain. And although doctors once described his heart as anatomically too small for his body, no one played with more heart and spirit. Despite his size, he was a gentle bear—indeed, when he broke into the NHL there were fears that he wasn't tough enough. But in 1955, he took on George Armstrong in a wicked fistfight and showed everyone he couldn't be intimidated.

The Canadiens fans loved Jean Beliveau and never showed it more than in the spring of 1968. It was the twilight of his career, and Beliveau had played brilliantly, scoring seven goals in nine games in playoff victories over the Boston Bruins and the Chicago Black Hawks. But in practice before the final series sweep against St. Louis, he broke his ankle. When the Stanley Cup was brought out for presentation, the Canadiens captain hobbled out on crutches and made a speech in French and English. The Forum reverberated with joy.

Big, graceful captain Jean Beliveau was able to fend off multiple defenders to make great plays at the net for the Canadiens.

MIKE BOSSY

Whether he was beating the crosstown rival Rangers or the Vancouver Canucks in the Stanley Cup finals, Mike Bossy became the most feared sniper in the NHL in the 1980s.

There has been no purer shooter in hockey history than the kid out of a cozy Montreal neighborhood.

Fifty goals is considered the high-water mark in a given season. Bossy is the only man to accomplish it nine successive times. Even the Great Gretzky didn't do it.

It seems unfathomable today, but fourteen other teams passed over Bossy in the 1977 draft. The reasoning is somewhat understandable. He was labeled a one-dimensional player: all shoot, no defense. No all-around play. Even when folks look back at Bossy's remarkable career, the emphasis is on how great a shooter he was and not on how great a player he was.

Forming a formidable partnership with Bryan Trottier, one of the game's top all-around centers, Bossy started scoring goals in bushels the moment he stepped into the NHL. The only reason he didn't pour in more than 573 was because he retired prematurely at age thirty-one with debilitating back problems. He was the most devastating weapon on a New York Islanders team that won four consecutive Stanley Cup titles from 1980 to 1983.

Bossy's shot was legendary for its lightning quickness. He seemed to possess a special sense that enabled him to know the exact location of the puck, the goalie, and the corner of the net at all times. Sometimes, he seemed to pop out of a hole in the ice, magically appear in the right circle, and convert one of Trottier's passes before the enemy goalie and defensemen had time to react.

Observers can argue about the velocity of players' shots, but one matter is beyond debate. No one could release the puck at the exact moment it hopped onto his stick like Mike Bossy. He was truly a sniper extraordinaire.

Bossy promised Islanders general manager Bill Torrey he was going to become the first rookie ever to score fifty goals in a season. He got fifty-three.

Bossy said he wanted to become the first player in thirty-six years to score fifty goals in fifty games. He put a ton of pressure on himself by pointing out it would be perhaps his greatest personal achievement. Only Maurice Richard—the great legend of Bossy's home city—had done it. Bossy didn't disappoint. After forty-seven games, he had forty-

Only a severe back problem stopped Mike Bossy from scoring more than 573 career goals.

eight goals. But in Games Forty-eight and Forty-nine, Calgary and Detroit shadowed him held him off the board. In Game Fifty against Quebec, he needed two goals. Nothing in the first period. Nothing in the second period. With five minutes remaining, the Islanders took to the power play. Suddenly, the puck was on Bossy's stick and he unleashed a backhander that beat Ron Grahame. With one minute and twenty-nine seconds remaining, Bossy uncorked a wicked wrist shot that beat Grahame again. Fifty in fifty!

Bossy's other attributes were often overlooked. He was a terrific skater. At six feet (182.8cm) and 185 pounds (84kg) he looked gaunt and thin, but he had a deceptive strength and showed great tenacity in battling away from checks and incessant clutching and grabbing.

He won the Calder Trophy for Rookie of the Year in 1978. He won the Conn Smythe Trophy for playoff MVP in 1982. He won the Lady Byng Trophy three times for outstanding and gentlemanly play. He could have won it ten times, for Mike Bossy was unafraid to speak out about how needless fighting was. He refused to tolerate it. He was a clean player. And in his finer moments, Bossy pointed out that no matter how many times somebody knocked him down, he'd get back up and score. That was his mark of a champion.

RAYMOND BOURQUE

Argue whether he is better at offense or at defense. Debate why Paul Coffey often got more attention early in their careers. Ponder the way he had to survive endless comparisons to another Boston defenseman who preceded him.

But don't ever question Raymond Bourque's durability and sustained greatness.

From the point he entered the NHL in 1979, nobody averaged more minutes played—except, of course, goalies. Only Gordie Howe, a right-winger, was selected for more NHL All-Star teams (first or second) than

Bourque. Howe was named to twelve first teams and nine second. Through 1994, Bourque was named to eleven first teams and four second. And only Paul Coffey scored more points among defensemen in a career.

It is true that Bobby Orr and Doug Harvey each won the Norris Trophy as the NHL's premier defenseman more times than Bourque's five. It is true that if there was a vote to name the best defenseman of all time, Bourque would not win. But in an era when too many athletes dog it, pull up because of injury, or allow their performance to waver, Bourque has been absolutely tireless in his pursuit of greatness. Mike Milbury, who played defense with Bourque, says Bourque was a chunky kid when he arrived from Verdun of the Quebec Junior Hockey League. Milbury wondered how dedicated he was. But Milbury said he found out about the size of Bourque's heart. Ray never wants to come off the ice. When he does, he sits on the bench only for a moment, gets up, and leaves a huge pool of perspiration behind.

Bourque may come to be the greatest defenseman never to win the Stanley Cup, but it isn't his fault. Twice, he went to the finals with the Bruins. Bourque's performance in Game One of the Stanley Cup championships in 1990 was priceless. He scored 2 goals in the third period to force overtime against the Edmonton Oilers. In one of the great Stanley Cup games in history, Petr Klima came off the bench in the third overtime to win it for the Oilers. Bourque logged a superhuman sixty minutes of ice time that night. Mark Messier won that year's Hart Trophy as the NHL's Most Valuable Player, but Bourque should have won it.

Except for goaltenders, nobody in hockey has logged more playing minutes since 1979 than Boston defenseman Raymond Bourque. He is a workhorse. He is a thoroughbred.

"That year, Ray played at a level no other defenseman had ever been at, bar none," says Milbury, who coached the Bruins in 1990. According to Rod Langway, himself a Norris Trophy winner, "No other defenseman in the NHL measures up to [Bourque] as a combination of offense and defense. Larry Robinson was like that in his prime. Paul Coffey is a great skater, a beautiful skater. But there's no comparison with Ray in his own end. He has such thick, strong legs, he should have been a linebacker in football. He just angles you and pushes you to the side."

Bourque reads plays as well as anyone in hockey and is a master of transition, turning the game from defense to offense. He knows when to clear the puck, when to pass tape-to-tape, and when to skate it out himself. Bourque is an excellent special teams player, adept at keeping the puck in at the point on the power play and utterly reliable in his end at killing penalties. And, always, there is his incredible skating balance. It would take a truck to knock him off the puck.

"Raymond is like Secretariat," said Hall of Fame goalie Gerry Cheevers, who coached Bourque during the 1980s. "He goes the full mile and a half."

Bourque is a gracious man, too. He gladly gave up his No. 7 for No. 77, so the Bruins could retire Phil Esposito's No. 7. Before the Boston Garden finally closed, Bourque had become as much a piece of the rickety Old Lady of Causeway as the parquet basketball floor, the cramped, undersized rink, and all those Celtic and Bruin banners that hung from the rafters.

BOBBY CLARKE

He had an angelic, gap-toothed grin. He wielded a devilish stick. And he was the greatest leader in the history of hockey.

Bobby Clarke's unique contribution to the sport did not lie with his hockey skills, which, although better than most, certainly did not pave the road to Clarke's two Stanley Cup championships with the Philadelphia Flyers and his entry into the Hall of Fame.

What set Clarke apart from the rest was his thirst for victory and an unparalleled zeal for the all-for-one-and-one-for-all team concept. Clarke possessed a profound enthusiasm that empowered not just himself, but everyone around him.

Clarke inspired greatness, commitment—and fear.

Diagnosed as a diabetic when he was thirteen, Clarke didn't play hockey three or four times a week in his northern Manitoba mining hometown of Flin Flon. He played every day. He didn't love hockey. He lived it. The game seemed to allow his cuts and bruises to heal faster than they should. His eyes were myopic, but only Wayne Gretzky ever displayed better hockey vision. His daily injection of insulin was neither a big deal nor an excuse. It was simply hockey regimen, the same as taping his sticks and lacing his skates.

Clarke excelled for his hometown junior club, the Flin Flon Bombers, but word of his diabetes seemed to cool some NHL interest. Clarke received medical clearance from the Mayo Clinic in Minnesota, assuring teams he would be healthy enough to play professional hockey.

Nevertheless, he lasted until seventeenth overall in the draft and some saw picking him as a gamble by the Flyers.

Some gamble! Clarke made the NHL immediately. He scored more than 100 points three times and he collected three Hart Trophies. When he retired in 1984, Clarke was the fourth-greatest assist man in NHL history.

But numbers were not what Clarke was about. When a team captures the Stanley Cup, inevitably the players are remembered as the most talented. The Flyers were not the most talented team of the mid-1970s, but they came away with two championships. It is true that these Broad Street Bullies used fists and intimidation. But in truth it was much more than that. With coach Fred Shero, a foggy professor who cited obscure quotations from Bartlett, and with Clarke leading passionately, no team was ever better focused on its task.

Clarke was unselfish. If a player carped about appearing free at a public appearance, Clarke would admonish his teammate to focus on something important. He watched over the rookies. When somebody went into a slump, he'd offer encouragement, even asking the coach to put the player on a line with him to improve the fellow's confidence.

Nor was Clarke without skill. He was an excellent passer, playmaker, and face-off man. His leverage and balance on his skates allowed him to snare the puck from bigger, stronger men.

But Clarke was also known to use his stick like a pitchfork. He knew teammates such as Dave Schultz, Don Saleski, and Moose Dupont would jump in at a second's notice to save him. He stuck his nose into deep dark places in a hockey rink, and in the end, he was as cut up as his opponent, his face a relief map of scars.

In fierce admiration of his unselfish play and relentless determination, Shero paid him the ultimate tribute: he called Clarke the only true athlete in modern sports.

Don't let that cherubic grin fool you. Bobby Clarke was one of the fiercest competitors in all of sports. That's why Philadelphia loved him so much.

KEN DRYDEN

Famous for his pose and for his prose, Ken Dryden was more than a great goalie: he is the poet laureate of the sport.

Many critics call the handful of goalies from the six-team Golden Era of the NHL the greatest in the game's history. They were guys who played with all sorts of guts, no masks, and no backup. Others prefer the more recent goalies, the young men with razor-sharp reflexes who nightly face the fastest, most potent offensive forces the game has seen.

There are some who will say this legendary goalie spot should be reserved for Jacques Plante or Patrick Roy. Critics may complain that Dryden fails the test of longevity, but there is so much more to Dryden that even the hallowed confines of the Montreal Forum cannot define his boundaries.

When he played, Dryden was famous for using his goalie stick as a support post during stoppages in play. He was resting, knowing Dryden's immense brain power, it was a pose that made him look pensive, not lazy.

At a time when virtually every NHL player was a product of Canada's major junior system, Dryden attended Cornell. He had turned down a chance to attend Harvard full time because he wanted to split his time between hockey and education. After gaining All-America, he turned down the Canadiens' offer to turn pro. Instead, he joined Canada's national team and began studying for a law degree at the University of Manitoba. Later, Dryden would join the Canadiens' minor league affiliate, the Montreal Voyageurs, while attending McGill University full time.

Not surprisingly, Dryden was a critic of the junior system, in which education was given little priority. Thankfully, because of people like Dryden, this has improved significantly during the last twenty years.

He was called up to the NHL for six games near the end of the 1970–71 season, where he allowed only nine goals. Amazingly, it was Dryden who got the call to start the playoffs instead of veteran Rogie Vachon.

Above: Dryden shows his winning form early in his career. Opposite: Resting on his stick so pensively, Dryden looked like Rodin's sculpture *The Thinker*. But once he started moving his six-foot-four (193cm) frame, opponents compared him to a giraffe or an octopus.

Ken Dryden's .751 winning percentage (258–57–74) is the best in NHL history among goalies with 200 wins.

Dryden was spectacular in the opening round, snuffing Boston. At that point, the Bruins were considered the greatest offensive machine in NHL history. At six feet four inches (193cm) Dryden was, in Phil Esposito's words, "a bleeping octopus."

The Canadiens went on to win the Stanley Cup. Dryden became the only man in NHL history to win the Conn Smythe Trophy for the NHL playoffs' Most Valuable Player before winning the Calder Trophy for Rookie of the Year.

From there, his numbers were staggering. Dryden posted a 258–57–74 record. His winning percentage of .758 is easily the best among NHL goalies with 200 career wins. In a little more than seven seasons, he had 46 shutouts and a 2.24 goals-against average. He led the Canadiens to six Stanley Cups, including four in a row. He was named first-team NHL All-Star five times. Despite the fact that Dryden played less than a decade, only Frank Brimsek and Glenn Hall were named more. In 1972, he backstopped Team Canada to its Summit Series victory over the Soviet Union.

Dryden stunned the hockey world before the 1973–74 season when he announced he was retiring to work for a Toronto law firm for $7,500 a year. He played for an industrial team in his spare time before returning to the NHL the following season. In 1979, he retired for good. He was only thirty-one. He went to England with his wife and children, and wrote a book. *The Game* was more than just another book about hockey. It furnished more insight into the sport and into the warriors who ply the ice than anything written before or after.

PHIL ESPOSITO

He did not own the most wicked slap shot in the world like Bobby Hull. He could not stickhandle like Wayne Gretzky. He could not grab the puck and play keep-away like Bobby Orr. He could not lift fans out of their seats like Maurice Richard and Guy Lafleur.

But until somebody changes the rules, the game is still won and lost on who scores the most goals. And Phil Esposito is one of only four men ever to score 700 goals in his career. When Esposito retired on January 9, 1981, with 717 goals, only the legendary Gordie Howe had more.

Esposito was called the ultimate garbageman; maybe he was—but this should be considered a mark of distinction, a badge of honor. Esposito doesn't have to apologize to anyone.

True, he could be lazy defensively. True, he didn't skate very quickly. He sometimes was accused of being selfish. But Esposito was not afraid to tread in front of the opposing net and park himself in the slot. When a player grows roots in front of the other team's goalie, he is considered fair game to clutches, grabs, slashes, and high-sticks from defensemen and the goalie. Esposito absorbed it all; over the years, he took some serious physical abuse.

Esposito led the NHL in scoring five times in a six-year period. He was the league's MVP in 1969 and 1974. Named first-team NHL center six times, he equaled both Jean Beliveau and Stan Mikita. Only Wayne Gretzky, with eight, has been the number one center more times in a career.

Some critics claim Esposito merely reaped the rewards of playing with such able cornermen as Ken Hodge and Wayne Cashman, not to mention the game's premier defenseman, Bobby Orr. The biggest rebuttal to that criticism is the 1972 Summit Series against the Soviets. Bobby Hull jumped to the World Hockey Association and didn't play. Orr couldn't play because of a knee injury. It is true that Paul Henderson, with 3 game-winning goals, was the storybook hero. But there is no denying that Esposito was Canada's best player in the classic showdown against the best hockey team Communism ever offered.

Esposito was born February 20, 1942, in Sault Ste. Marie, Ontario. The older brother of Tony Esposito, who became one of the top goalies in NHL history, Phil got to be the shooter for a simple reason: Phil was bigger and older, and it's more fun to shoot the puck.

The Chicago Blackhawks had his rights from the time he was a youth because they sponsored the hockey program in Esposito's hometown, affectionately known as "the Soo." Called up to the NHL in 1963, Esposito labored on his skates and scored only 3 goals in 27 rookie games. He centered Bobby Hull for a time and ended up with 71 goals in three seasons. Not spectacular stats, but Hull did lead the NHL in goals during that period.

Esposito's life changed drastically in May 1967 when the Hawks traded Fred Stanfield, Esposito, and Hodge to Boston for Pit Martin, Gilles Marotte, and Jack Norris. It may have been the most one-sided trade in NHL history.

Esposito's point totals grew in leaps and bounds. He became the first NHL player to score 100 points when he got 126 in 1968–69, and his 76 goals and 152 points in 1970–71 stood for a decade until Gretzky came along. Esposito was traded to the Rangers in a deal on November 7, 1975, that sent Jean Ratelle and Brad Park to the Bruins. Esposito never again was the game's dominant force, but he did settle in as a fan favorite in the Big Apple. Perhaps a bumper sticker that found its way onto many cars in New England in the early 1970s best describes his career: "Jesus saves! And Esposito scores on the rebound!"

Maybe his goals weren't always pretty. But whether in a Bruins or Rangers jersey, Phil Esposito took the abuse in the slot and displayed an uncanny knack for scoring goals.

WAYNE GRETZKY

Watch Wayne Gretzky skate once and it is easy to see how he became the greatest play-maker in hockey history.

Watch Wayne Gretzky ten times and you begin to understand how a reed-thin kid who had neither the strongest body nor the hardest shot could nevertheless become the greatest goal scorer the game has ever seen.

But skills tell only part of Gretzky's story. Over fifteen years, slowly, surely, Gretzky won over every doubter, cynic, and wise guy. His nickname, the Great One, seems almost understated today.

Gretzky's first pro contract, for $875,000 over four years, was signed with the Indianapolis Racers of the World Hockey Association in 1978. The team fell to financial woes, and the owner of the Edmonton Oilers, Peter Pocklington, bought Gretzky's contract for $850,000.

Many doubted whether the center could rewrite NHL record books as he had done everywhere else he had gone. After all, the NHL was a man's league—only the rough and powerful survived. The rough and powerful, however, soon found that they couldn't hit what they couldn't catch. Gretzky didn't score 378 goals in 85 games like he did when he was ten years old, but darned if there weren't some seasons when it looked as if he might.

He scored 50 goals in 39 games in 1981–82 on his way to a record 92 goals and 212 points. In 1985–86, he snapped two of his own records with 163 assists and 215 points. Gretzky has led the NHL in scoring ten times. He won the Hart Trophy nine times as league MVP, including an eight-in-a-row stretch. He won the Conn Smythe Trophy as playoff MVP twice. And there were special moments:

•On December 30, 1981, Gretzky scored 5 goals against Philadelphia to hit the 55-goal mark in 49 games.

•On February 24, 1982, he scored on Don Edwards in Buffalo to break Phil Esposito's single-season record of 76 goals.

•On November 22, 1986, he surpassed Mike Bossy's record for scoring 500 goals in a career in the shortest time.

•On October 15, 1989, he scored on Bill Ranford in Edmonton to set the all-time point record, surpassing Gordie Howe.

•On March 2, 1994, he beat Kirk McLean for his 802nd goal, surpassing Howe's all-time record. Gretzky's first goal had been against Vancouver on October 14, 1979.

Even the circumstances of his trade were the most spectacular in the history of the sport. On August 9, 1988, in a move intended to patch up his personal finances, Pocklington traded Gretzky and three other

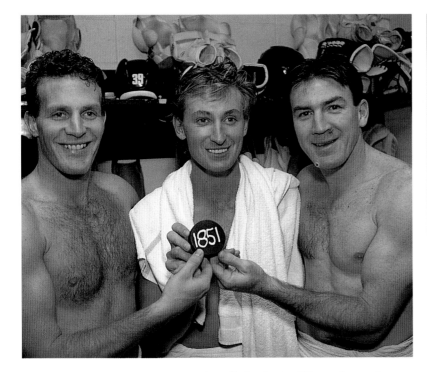

players to Los Angeles' Bruce McNall for $15 million, three players, and three first-round draft picks.

Gretzky not only scored more and set up more goals than anybody else, he also took the sport on his slender six-foot (182.8), 170-pound (77.1kg) build and lifted it to another level.

Gretzky was a magnet. Everywhere he went, the fans were sure to go. He filled arenas not only in longtime hockey havens but everywhere across North America. He led the Edmonton Oilers to four Stanley Cup championships. Later, he ignited the hockey flame on the West Coast that saw him not only pace the Los Angeles Kings to the Stanley Cup finals but also pave the way for NHL expansion in Anaheim and San Jose, California.

And whenever a special moment of achievement was at hand, whether he was leading the Oilers to the Stanley Cup or breaking one of Gordie Howe's records, he remained gracious and accessible. His dad, Walter, who had flooded the backyard to make a rink not long after Gretzky was born in 1961 in Brantford, Ontario, remained a trusted companion. In addition, Gretzky always paid homage to the great Gordie Howe; indeed, they became good friends when it would have been just as easy not to.

Through 1994, Gretzky held a dizzying sixty-one NHL individual records. But, in truth, there is no tangible way to sum up how much he has done for the sport.

The number 99 became as well known as his name. Wayne Gretzky won championships in Edmonton, sold hockey to the West Coast, and set scoring record after scoring record.

Gretzky's tearful 1988 farewell to the Oilers was obviously a sad moment for the Great One—and to many Canadians, it was a national tragedy—nevertheless, his move to Los Angeles turned out well both for the player himself and the game in general.

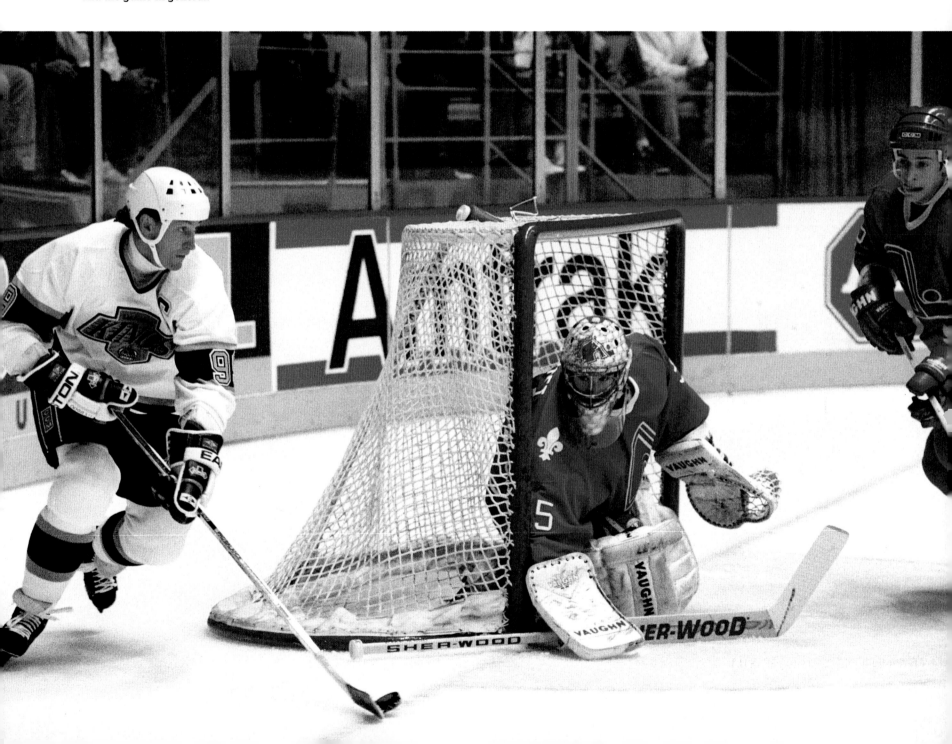

GLENN HALL

The end came at 10:21 of the first period on November 7, 1962. Agonized by a back injury, Chicago Black Hawks goalie Glenn Hall pulled himself out of a game against Boston and ended the most incredible iron man story in hockey history.

Hall played 552 consecutive games in goal, including 502 in the regular season. That added up to 33,135 successive minutes of unrelenting pressure. The painful sacroiliac condition that forced him out of the Boston game was caused by the stiff new pads Hall had tried out in practice the day before.

Night after night, month after month, season after season, Hall, who became known as Mr. Goalie, subjected himself to the strain of goaltending. Goalies didn't wear masks in those days. Injury was a constant threat. For any goalie to perform so brilliantly for 552 games surely indicates how much he loved to play. Right?

Wrong. Hall admitted to hating every minute he played. He used to get sick before games and inbetween periods. Vomiting was as much a part of Hall's game as was the "butterfly" goaltending technique he first perfected. Hall used words like "torture" to describe his craft.

For every training camp, Hall seemed slow to show up from his Alberta farm. The word was always that Hall was painting his barn. The reason he took so long to arrive was because his head and heart were reluctant to undergo another season of punishment. Yet from 1955 until 1962, he never missed a minute.

Hall hailed from Humboldt, Saskatchewan, where he grew up playing hockey on the outdoor ice surfaces of that tiny railway center. His dad was a railroad engineer. As a schoolboy, Hall played forward. But one day the goalie got hurt. As captain of the team, Hall tried to persuade each boy on the team to play goalie. Nobody would. So Hall put

Glenn Hall (shown during the 1992—93 season) played 552 consecutive games in goal and later became a goalie-coach.

Glenn Hall demonstrated an endurance that made him a legend in the crease.

on the pads, and much to his chagrin, he never left the crease. He perfected the butterfly style, in which he would drop to his knees and fan out his pads to cover as much net as possible while still being able to use his glove and stick.

Hall broke into the NHL with Detroit in 1955, pushing another goalie legend, Terry Sawchuk, out of a job. Hall played all 70 games his rookie season, winning the Calder Trophy for Rookie of the Year. He was traded in 1957, because Detroit general manager Jack Adams did not like his style. Oddly enough, Hall had just given a glimpse of his courage in the semifinals against Boston. After Vic Stasiuk had caught him full in the face with a shot, Hall, barely conscious, was carted off the ice. He took twenty-five stitches to the lip and mouth, yet returned later that game.

Hall was named an NHL first-team All-Star seven times and second-team All-Star four times—the most in the league's history for a goalkeeper.

Hall's career hit its zenith in 1961 when the Black Hawks captured their first Stanley Cup in twenty-three years. Hall was brilliant in the playoffs. At one point, he held the Montreal Canadiens scoreless for 136 minutes. Rocket Richard had retired, but these were the Canadiens who had just won five Stanley Cups in a row and counted Jean Beliveau and Bernie "Boom Boom" Geoffrion among their forces.

Hall was ready to retire in 1967 when the St. Louis Blues selected him in the expansion draft. A $45,000 salary—the highest ever at that time for a goalie—persuaded him to keep playing. Hall led the Blues to the Stanley Cup finals and was named playoff MVP.

DOUG HARVEY

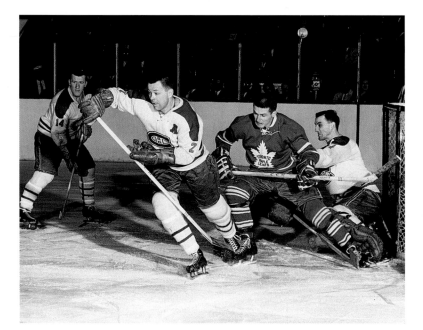

Montreal defenseman Doug Harvey made it look easy, and sometimes he took it so easy he infuriated his coaches and fans. The fact remains that Harvey, the rebel, was one of the three or four best defensemen in history.

When everybody else was panicking on the ice, Doug Harvey seemed to be on a leisurely Sunday skate. When the play turned frantic, he turned the flow down two notches. But when the play turned sleepy, he'd set off the alarms, bells, and whistles on the Montreal Canadiens' legendary firewagon hockey style.

If matters turned too serious in the locker room, Harvey was known to break up everybody with a gag. When everybody else was toeing the line to management, he became a rebel in the players' association. He also acted as player–head coach of the New York Rangers for one year, although he was a man known to have trouble disciplining himself away from the ice.

Harvey was a study in contradictions. But there are two matters upon which everyone seems to agree. He was his own man. And he was the best defenseman after Eddie Shore and before Bobby Orr. His own coach, Hector "Toe" Blake, who handled Harvey when the Canadiens reeled off their record five successive Stanley Cup championships in the 1950s, called Harvey the greatest defenseman ever.

But that doesn't mean his style didn't drive fans, coaches, and even his teammates crazy. At times, fans thought he was loafing, that his mind was on fishing or carousing. Described as playing hockey like he was in a rocking chair, Harvey earned the nickname Lazy Lightning. He would gain control of the puck and casually stickhandle around, daring anybody to steal it. It was rare that someone did. Instead, Harvey would draw a defender out of position and deftly send in one of his forwards racing on goal with a splendid tape-to-tape pass.

Harvey was a terrific athlete. As a young man, he played minor league football with his hometown Montreal Hornets. Many were convinced he had Major League Baseball talent. The Boston Braves drafted Harvey, but he refused to play in the low minors. He stuck with hockey, and it was a wise choice.

Harvey was a strong, tough player but not known to be wicked. Nevertheless, in 1956, he almost killed another player. Red Sullivan had a bad habit of kicking out skates—especially from under Harvey. Harvey warned Sullivan repeatedly but Sullivan didn't listen. One night, Harvey had had enough and stabbed Sullivan in the gut with the point of his stick blade. Shockingly, Sullivan suffered a ruptured spleen and was in serious enough condition to be given last rites before he finally recovered.

The Norris Trophy was instituted in 1954 to honor the NHL's outstanding defenseman. Red Kelly won it the first year, but Harvey won it seven of the next eight years.

The Canadiens' power play was so dynamic in the 1950s that the NHL devised a rule that an offending player could come back on the ice after one power-play goal instead of serving the full two minutes. Granted, Rocket Richard, Jean Beliveau, and Boom Boom Geoffrion amassed the goals. But it was Harvey who choreographed the brilliance. His biggest fault was that he didn't shoot enough. But to this criticism he simply retorted: why shoot when you've got the Rocket and Boom Boom as teammates?

The Canadiens released Harvey after contract hassles. His relationship with the Rangers ended because he wanted to hang out and have a few beers with the players and not be a coach. He kicked around in the minors for a number of years before resurfacing in his forties with the St. Louis Blues. Harvey had a way of irritating the hockey establishment. And the hockey establishment callously struck back, choosing not to induct him into the Hall of Fame until 1983—fourteen years after he retired.

1956 was an exciting year for Harvey and the Canadiens—it marked the start of a five-in-a-row Stanley Cup streak.

GORDIE HOWE

The legendary Howe played long enough to earn several nicknames—early on, he was known as Blinky because of a tic that resulted from a near-tragic hockey accident. Later, his teammates called him Power because of his raw strength. Decades later, he was Gramps—he played so long that he was a grandfather when he finally retired in 1980.

But there is only one name truly worthy of Gordie Howe. It is Mr. Hockey.

He skated off the plains of Saskatchewan and into the NHL in 1946 at age eighteen. The boys were just coming home from World War II. Harry Truman was president. When Howe finally retired at age 52, it was April 1980. He played thirty-two years of profession-al hockey in five decades. Including playoffs and his stint in the World Hockey Association, he played in 2,421 games and scored 1,071 goals and 2,589 points.

Born in Floral, Saskatchewan, in 1928, Howe was a Depression baby. He used hand-me-down skates and broken sticks. For shin pads, he used magazine catalogs. But he was to become as famous in Detroit as Joe Louis or any one of the Tigers or Lions. Oddly enough, he could have been a New York Ranger. A thin and wiry kid, the homesick Howe was sent home from Rangers training camp. Fred Pinkney, a Red Wings scout, tipped off Jack Adams. Howe got a Red Wings jacket as part of his signing bonus and earned $2,600 his rookie season.

Howe scored his first NHL goal on October 16, 1946. Officially, the NHL record book will show Howe scored 801 goals. But including the WHA and the playoffs, he was the first man ever to score 1,000 goals

when on December 7, 1977, in Birmingham, Alabama, of all places, he beat the Bulls' John Garrett.

But there was a moment in 1950 when it almost all ended for Howe. Trying to take out Ted Kennedy during a playoff game, Howe missed. Kennedy stopped short. Howe rammed into the boards and fractured his skull. He was close to death. His parents were called in from Canada while surgeons operated to relieve the pressure on his brain. He recovered, but the injury left Howe with the aforementioned tic and nickname.

In 1959, it was Lou Fontinato of the Rangers—considered the game's toughest fighter at that time—doing the blinking. Fontinato wanted Howe, but when Gordie was finished with him, Fontinato had a broken nose and his face was a mess. It was one of the most memorable fights in NHL history.

Howe's sloped shoulders were the trademark tip-off to his extraor-dinary strength. A well-placed Howe elbow left many a daring player flattened in NHL corners. Howe was ambidextrous: he could stickhan-dle with either hand. And when one arm was tied up by checkers, he could switch hands and shoot lefty.

In all, Howe won the Hart Trophy six times. He led the NHL in scoring six times. He was named either first- or second-team All-Star right wing an amazing twenty-one times. In Howe's heyday, the Red Wings finished in first place during the regular season seven times in a row, and Howe gained fame with the Production Line of Sid Abel and Ted Lindsay.

In his heyday in Detroit, nobody wanted to go into the corners with Gordie Howe. His elbows were legendary. His strength was extraordinary.

Howe tried retirement in 1971. He hated it. He said he was the Red Wings vice president in charge of paper clips. He said he got the mushroom treatment: they kept him in the dark and occasionally opened the door to shove manure on him. So he accepted Bill Dineen's call to join the Houston Aeros of the WHA in 1973. Joined by his sons Mark and Marty, Howe and the Aeros won two Avco Cups. All three went to Hartford in 1976. "It legitimized our franchise," said former Whalers owner Howard Baldwin. It also gave Howe one final season in the NHL when the WHA teams merged with the senior league in 1979–80.

No less a luminary than Jean Beliveau called Howe the best hockey player he'd ever seen. And Rocket Richard agreed that Howe was a better all-around performer. Is Howe better than Bobby Orr and Wayne Gretzky, too? Most hockey experts argue that since Orr's career was cut short by knee problems, Howe gets the edge. The Gretzky versus Howe argument will be waged for decades. Although Gretzky has broken Howe's scoring records, nobody can touch Howe's longevity marks. Jack Adams, who ran the Detroit Red Wings with an iron fist for years, once said: "Hockey has had many superstars. But it has had only one superman. And that's Gordie Howe."

He began his career in 1946 in Detroit, and after retiring once, Gordie Howe returned to star in the World Hockey Association with Houston and Hartford. When his legendary career had ended, his sons were his teammates and Gordie was a grandfather.

BOBBY HULL

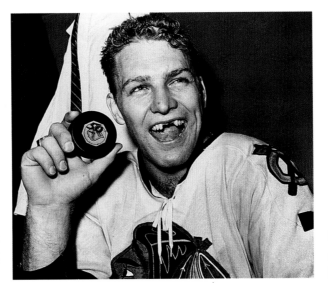

The Golden Jet. It was the perfect nickname, the perfect description of Bobby Hull.

His name became synonymous with the term "slap shot." He used his powerful legs, barrel chest, and Popeye arms to wind up and propel a puck like no man before or after him. In his prime, at five feet ten inches (177.8cm) and 195 pounds (88.5kg), Hull was the NHL's fastest skater and hardest shooter.

Hull used a blade curved like a banana. In years to come, his type of stick would be banned. It is an understatement to say that Hull struck fear in the hearts of goalies. With that curve and his power, he could take a goalie's head off. His rising slapper was once timed at 118 miles per hour (188.8kph). Whenever he touched the puck, a crescendo of oohs and aahs filled the hockey arena.

Toss in that flowing blond hair of his youth and his presence with the fans and it was small wonder why Hull was an idol to millions. The man signed autographs for hours.

Hull came from Pointe Anne, Ontario, where he got ice skates as a Christmas present when he was four years old. His sisters Maxine and Laura taught him to skate. As he grew older, he spent hours clearing the snow from the Bay of Quinte so he could play shinny hockey. In the summer, he worked on relatives' farms, chopping trees, putting up fences, and digging irrigation ditches. He developed into a rock and was a star on the high school football team, too.

Hull quit junior hockey when he was only eighteen to turn pro with the Chicago Black Hawks. He had already undergone one great transformation. While playing for the St. Catharines TeePees, coached by Rudy Pilous, Hull was suspended for indifferent play and for hogging the puck. He went home, but Hull's dad convinced him that Pilous was right. Hull returned and apologized to Pilous and his teammates. On that day, the boy with the powerhouse physique became a man.

Hull went on to become the NHL's first $100,000-a-year player. Ten times he was NHL first-team left-winger. He led the league in scoring three times. He was MVP twice. In the years preceding the NHL's expansion from six to twelve teams, Hull was the NHL's most dynamic player. His brother Dennis was also a fine player. And years later, Bobby's son, Brett, would follow in his dad's footsteps, scoring 86 goals in 1991.

Goalies lived in fear of Hull's slapshot. On March 25, 1962, Hull slammed the puck past the Rangers' Gump Worsley to become the third man in NHL history to score 50 goals in a season.

Two moments define exactly how dynamic Hull was.

In 1966, Maurice Richard, Bernie Geoffrion, and Hull were the only players to have scored 50 goals in a season. This was to change on March 12, when twenty-one thousand fans—four thousand above capacity—jammed Chicago Stadium for a game against the Rangers.

At 4:05 of the third period, Harry Howell of the Rangers was called for slashing. Hull went to the point on the power play. The Hawks had no luck for almost ninety seconds until Lou Angotti sent the puck ahead to Hull. Hull slowed down a bit, allowing his teammates to catch up. Eric Nesterenko headed to the net for distraction. Angotti tipped goalie Cesare Maniago's stick. Maniago braced for a Hull slap shot. But instead of a mighty blast, Hull took a wrist shot for goal number 51. What followed at 5:34 of the third period may have been the most stunning fan response in hockey history: a seven-and-a-half-minute standing ovation.

But many argue that Hull's greatest impact on hockey took place away from the ice. On June 27, 1972, he jumped from the Black Hawks to the Winnipeg Jets of the new World Hockey Association. He signed a previously unheard of $2.75 million contract, including $1 million up front. The other WHA teams chipped in just to get Hull into their league. Playing with super Swedes Anders Hedberg and Ulf Nilsson, Hull scored as many as 77 goals in one season. In all, he finished with 610 NHL and 303 WHA goals. In a strange twist, Hull played his final hockey game as a teammate of Gordie Howe in 1980 with the Hartford Whalers of the NHL.

The fans loved to watch The Golden Jet roar. With his blond hair, powerful stride, and barrel chest, Bobby Hull was a devastating sight.

After jumping to the World Hockey Association and legitimizing that rebel league with the
Winnipeg Jets, Bobby Hull finished his NHL career with a brief fling with Gordie Howe in Hartford.

GUY LAFLEUR

His last name translates literally to *the flower*. And nobody in hockey history could ever have been better named.

Guy Lafleur took three full years to bloom in the NHL, but when he was finished he was a beautiful hockey player to behold—indeed, he was the greatest player of the second half of the 1970s.

Lafleur did not sneak into the NHL. By the time he burst into junior hockey, he was already recognized as a rising star. He scored 130 goals and 209 points his last season with the Quebec Remparts. Not since Jean Beliveau had French Canada so eagerly waited for one of their own to enter the major leagues.

The Montreal Canadiens wanted Lafleur dearly. The Canadiens had won the Stanley Cup in 1971. California finished last. Through a complicated web of negotiations, Sam Pollock, the Canadiens' shrewd general manager, ended up with the California Golden Seals' first-round pick. Somehow Pollock had wheeled and dealed his way into getting the game's greatest young player. At the draft table, Pollock, ordinarily a stern sort, kiddingly called time-out when his team was called to make their selection. Everybody in the hockey world knew he'd take Lafleur.

This was the same year Beliveau retired from the Canadiens. The torch would be passed directly to Lafleur. It was perfect—that is, except for one small matter. Lafleur wasn't ready to be a star. The first season he scored 64 points, the second 55, and the third 56. Labeled a bust in Montreal, Lafleur became a nervous wreck, even contemplating playing for Quebec in the World Hockey Association. But suddenly in 1974, Lafleur's immense talents kicked in. He reeled off seasons of 119, 125, 135, 132, 129, and 125 points. He scored at least 50 goals in all six of those seasons. He led the NHL in scoring three successive years during that span, something no Canadien had done before.

The Canadiens won the Stanley Cup four times from 1976 to 1979. Lafleur won the Hart Trophy twice as the NHL's Most Valuable Player during that time and in 1977 he was named MVP of the playoffs. He scored 36 goals and had 51 assists in 58 playoff games on those four marches to the Cup, a dizzying pace of almost 1.5 points a game.

Lafleur was a study in speed, determination, and artistry as he raced down the right wing, pushed the puck through an enemy defenseman's legs, popped out the other side, and beat the goalie with a wicked slap shot all in one devastating motion. Yes, Ken Dryden was a brilliant goalie. The Big Three on defense, Serge Savard, Larry Robinson, and Guy Lapointe, were nearly impenetrable. Bob Gainey may have been the greatest defensive forward in history. But with Jacques Lemarie centering his line, Lafleur was the scoring dynamo. To his fans he was like the Roman god Mercury.

Opposite: It took a few years for The Flower to bloom, but Guy Lafleur grew into the great offensive force and dynamic performer the fans loved at Montreal Forum. Above: Guy Lafleur scored his 500th goal on December 20, 1983, against the New Jersey Devils.

His greatest score came in the closing moments of Game Seven of the 1979 semifinals against Boston. It was the result of perhaps the most famous penalty in hockey history. With only two minutes left and ahead by a goal, the Bruins, incredibly, were caught with too many men on the ice. With one minute and fourteen seconds remaining, Lemaire slid the puck over to the right wing. With stick already pulled back, Lafleur hit with one touch a bullet behind goalie Gilles Gilbert and into the far corner. The Canadiens would win in overtime and go on to capture their fourth Stanley Cup in a row.

Lafleur was inducted into the Hockey Hall of Fame in 1988. But he came out of retirement to play three more seasons with the Rangers and Nordiques. His old greatness was gone, but he didn't embarrass himself.

MARIO LEMIEUX

At six feet four inches (193cm) and 210 pounds (95.3kg), and blessed with immeasurable skills, Mario Lemieux has more weapons in his arsenal than anyone who has ever played hockey. If Wayne Gretzky could be compared to Magic Johnson, Lemieux could be compared to Michael Jordan.

The Great Gretzky is the consummate playmaker. Le Magnifique is the ultimate game breaker.

But fate has not been kind to Lemieux. Indeed, he may have been robbed of becoming the greatest player in hockey history. Just at the point in his career when he appeared truly unstoppable, Lemieux had to step out of the game. His will to play was there; unfortunately, his body rebelled.

Through his first decade in the NHL, Lemieux played 599 games, missing 201 because of injury. On August 29, 1994, Lemieux announced he would sit out an entire season for health reasons. He had been dogged by chronic back problems, and he was recently diagnosed with Hodgkin's disease.

When he entered the NHL, there were whispers from detractors hacking away at his hockey genius. Sure, he had incredible talent, the critics would say, but he's lazy, he doesn't play defense, he turns it on one night and off the next.

Lemieux did not sneak up on the NHL. When you score 133 goals and 282 points in your final year of junior hockey, your talents don't remain a secret. There is still much discussion among hockey observers whether the Pittsburgh Penguins went in the tank in the 1983–84 season in order to drop below the New Jersey Devils and get their shot at drafting Lemieux.

Lemieux scored 100 points as a rookie and just kept on scoring. With 494 goals in 599 games before his self-imposed exile, Lemieux had the highest goals-per-game ratio in NHL history: .825. His record of 2.022 points per game is second only to Gretzky's.

Despite Lemieux's success, there were still some who griped that all Lemieux could do was score in bunches in home games or against weak opponents. The critics were silenced when Lemieux led the Penguins to back-to-back Stanley Cup titles in 1991 and 1992. Both times, Lemieux, who also has two Hart Trophies as MVP and four Ross Trophies as leading scorer, won the Conn Smythe Trophy as outstanding performer in the playoffs.

Lemieux's one-on-one moves are unparalleled. He has an uncanny ability to wrestle his arm and stick free from an opponent's grasp. Like Gordie Howe, Lemieux is strong enough to muscle away from any defenseman. Like Gretzky, he is a master stickhandler.

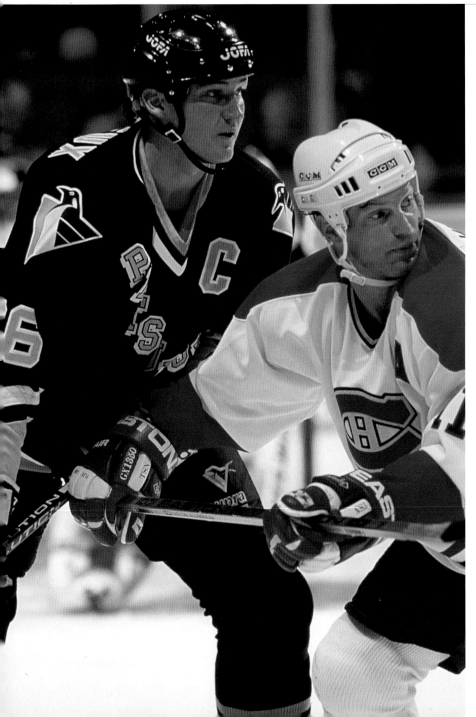

His size, strength, and skill made Mario Lemieux nearly unstoppable. He did more than save hockey in Pittsburgh. He brought the Iron City Stanley Cups in 1991 and 1992.

In 1987, Lemieux and Gretzky played on the same line in the Canada Cup tournament against the Soviet Union. It was the best hockey ever played. Gretzky set a tournament record for assists. Lemieux, who scored the final 2 game winners in dramatic fashion, set the record for goals. He scored as many as 85 goals and 199 points in a single NHL season.

It all should have kept rolling from there. But Lemieux was unable to enjoy his seven-year, $42 million contract.

After overcoming fierce back pain in the 1989–90 season, he underwent surgery to remove a herniated disc on July 11, 1990. But an infection stemming from the procedure kept him out until January 26, 1991. Lemieux overcame a fractured hand from a vicious slash by the Rangers' Adam Graves to lead the Penguins to the Stanley Cup in 1992. He had another back operation on July 28, 1993. Then he was diagnosed with Hodgkin's disease and underwent radiation treatments. The disease is in remission, and when Lemieux recovers from the treatments, hockey fans will welcome him back.

At the point in his career when Lemieux was poised to state his argument that he was the greatest player who ever lived, ill health dragged him down.

MARK MESSIER

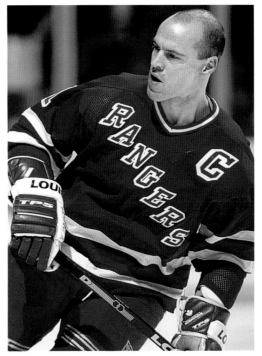

To call him the ultimate power forward and leave it at that is to do Mark Messier an injustice. To recall that he has won six Stanley Cup championships in an era when it has become much more difficult to repeat once does not tell the whole tale either.

The Mark Messier story is told in his eyes. Only the immortal Rocket Richard had a stare so fierce, so unrelenting. After one look into those eyes, his teammates swore they knew Messier would lead them to greatness in the most crucial situations. Another look into those eyes and teammates swore they were too afraid to let Messier down.

When Messier finally retires, however, he will be remembered for having all the attributes of a power forward.

Can he skate? Like the cold Alberta wind.

Can he shoot? His wrist shot is a canon and he doesn't need time to unleash it. He shoots in full stride.

Does he forecheck? Does he backcheck? Does he bodycheck? Check. Check. Check.

He is muscular. At six feet one inch (185.4cm) and 210 pounds (95.3kg), he is made of bedrock. It is only because of his talent that Messier doesn't need to fight or waste his energy on physical play. But he could if he had to.

His career didn't start out so smoothly. Messier was only seventeen when he signed with Indianapolis of the World Hockey Association. The team soon folded, forcing him to finish his first professional season with the Cincinnati Stingers. He was hardly a success. He scored 1 goal in 52 games and that was on a shot from center ice.

Messier was from the Edmonton area. And when the Oilers entered the NHL, Glen Sather made Messier his second pick in the 1979 draft. And what a draft it was for the Oilers. They took Kevin Lowe, Messier, and Glenn Anderson that day.

Messier progressed rapidly. He was named NHL first-team All-Star left wing twice and second-team once. He scored 50 goals in 1981–82.

But he also operated in the shadow of Wayne Gretzky. And when Messier moved to center to lead the Oilers' number two line, he took a backseat to Number 99. But it is indicative of Messier's importance to the Oilers that when they fell to the Islanders in the 1983 Stanley Cup finals, Messier was suffering from a bad shoulder.

In 1984, he was healthy. The Oilers won the Stanley Cup, and Messier was named playoff MVP. Many agree that one special moment put the Oilers over the top. With the finals against the Islanders tied at

It's in his eyes. Not since Maurice Richard in the 1950s did a cold stare from a player so inspire and scare teammates to greatness as one from Mark Messier.

1 and the Oilers behind 2–1 in Game Three, Messier blew away Gord Dineen with a move and whipped a shot behind goalie Billy Smith. The Oilers won the game 5–2 and rushed to their first Cup.

Messier and Gretzky won three more Stanley Cups together. And after Gretzky was traded, Messier responded by winning his first Hart Trophy in 1990 and leading the Oilers to their fifth Stanley Cup in seven seasons.

In 1991 Messier got caught up in Edmonton's housecleaning of big salaries. He was shipped to the Rangers and, true to form, immediately responded by capturing another Hart Trophy in 1992. But it was in 1994 that Messier became the toast of New York when the hockey world watched with awe as he led the Rangers to their first Stanley Cup in fifty-four years.

When matters looked bleak before Game Six of the Stanley Cup semifinals in New Jersey, Messier boldly predicted victory. For half the game he failed to live up to his own words. But, suddenly, he scored. And then again. And again. Messier had a hat trick. The Rangers won that night and went on to take the Stanley Cup. The New York tabloids crowned Messier the Messiah.

Mark Messier brought new meaning to the term power forward. He is a swift, powerful skater, capable of a terrific shot in full stride. He also can bounce bodies and instill fear.

HOWIE MORENZ

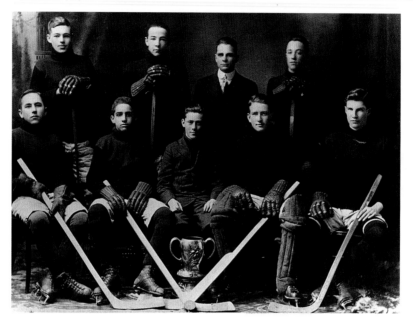

One hears the nickname "the Babe Ruth of Hockey" and assumes the topic of praise is Gordie Howe. Wrong. It was actually Howie Morenz who carried that tag during the 1920s and early 1930s—for all the right reasons.

Howarth William Morenz lived life fast both on and off the ice. He was a dynamic skater and flamboyant offensive star. He had a love affair with the city of Montreal and the city of Montreal had a love affair with him.

If Eddie Shore, the rock of Boston, was the greatest defensive player of hockey's first generation, Morenz was its premier offensive force.

Don't let the total of 270 career goals fool you. This was an era of greatly reduced schedules, when goals were precious. In 1929–30, for example, Morenz scored 40 goals in 44 games. Paired with another great, Aurel Joliat, the two gave meaning to the term Flying Frenchmen.

Morenz's blurring moves and wicked shot earned him the nickname the Stratford Streak. He was born in Mitchell, Ontario, in 1902, but moved thirteen miles (20.8km) to Stratford at age nine. As a teenager,

he scored 9 goals in one game, thereby attracting the attention of Montreal's Leo Dandurand.

Morenz, a five-foot-nine-inch (175.2cm), 165-pound (74.9kg) center, shot to prominence during a time when Babe Ruth, Jack Dempsey, Bobby Jones, and Bill Tilden reigned in America. The French Canadians praised him as *l'homme eclair*. This has nothing to do with chocolate pastry. It meant top man. Everybody claimed him. He was also known as the Mitchell Meteor and the Canadian Comet. He became the first player to win the Hart Trophy three times as the league's MVP. In 1931, he scored the Stanley Cup winning goal in the decisive game of the finals.

Like Ruth, Morenz played hard, lived hard, and laughed often. He was known to sleep only a few hours a night. He took losing so hard that he'd pace the streets half the night, brooding. After a victory, he'd dance through those same streets. He never stood still.

He played the ukulele. He wore spats. Fancying himself a fashion plate, he changed his clothes two or three times a day. The English-speaking fans loved his fiery play. The French-speaking fans loved his

Opposite, front row, far left, Howie Morenz in 1917. Right: Later in his career, Morenz knew something about painting Old Montreal red. He lived hard and fast. He also was the best offensive player in the first half of the twentieth century.

flair. And, then, one day in 1934, it all began to burn out. He was traded to Chicago. It didn't work out. He was traded to the Rangers. It didn't work out in New York, either. His legs were going. In 1936, Cecil Hart brought Morenz back to the Canadiens. At thirty-four, he wasn't the same player he had been six or seven years earlier, but periodically he'd perform brilliantly and thrill his fans.

Then on January 28, 1937, while trying to whirl behind Chicago's Earl Seibert with a one-on-one move, Morenz was hit by Seibert. It was a clean check, but Morenz went feet-first into the boards. The point of his skate blade stuck into the wood and Morenz rolled over, suffering an ugly compound fracture.

His life, if not his career, should have gone on. But Morenz did not recover at Hospital Saint-Luc. Thoughts of his career ending haunted him. He sulked. Some say he did not rest because of too many visitors. On March 8, 1937, he died of cardiac failure. His body lay in state at center ice in Montreal Forum. At the funeral service, fifteen thousand people sat in total silence. An estimated 100,000 lined the streets of Montreal as the funeral procession rolled from the Forum to the cemetery. Hockey had lost its first superstar.

BOBBY ORR

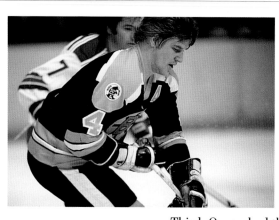

Number 4. Bobby Orr.

When those words blared over the public-address system at rickety old Boston Garden, they did more than rhyme. They were a lyrical introduction to a man who lifted hockey to a higher level. Only two or three others could ever make that claim.

Number four is fitting in another sense. For there are four areas in which Orr will not be forgotten.

First, Orr revolutionized the position of defense. Sure, Eddie Shore and a couple of other great defensemen before Orr did grab the puck and rush up the ice with it. But nobody ever did it with the grace, élan, and sheer drama of this kid from Parry Sound, Ontario.

Orr led the Boston Bruins' attack like no defenseman in the history of the sport. He jumped into the play, stickhandled through opponents as if they were standing still, and either drove a low, hard shot behind a goalie or dished the puck off to his corps of talented forwards.

As a result, the Bruins had become the most feared offensive machine in the NHL by 1970.

Orr had his detractors. He didn't pay enough attention to his defensive end. Dallas Smith had to bail him out defensively on many nights. He didn't eliminate men in front of his own net with much gusto. But none of the criticism stopped Orr from racking up an incredible eight Norris Trophies in a row as outstanding NHL defenseman. He was the first player in NHL history to win four individual trophies in one season in 1970. In addition to the Norris, he won the Ross (scoring title), Hart (league MVP), and Smythe (playoff MVP) as he led the Bruins to their first of two Stanley Cups in a three-year period.

Second, Orr captured the hearts of millions of New Englanders. There were thousands of kids across a six-state region who pretended they were Bobby Orr as they skated across local ponds and rinks. Every time a kid came along who played defense and showed any offensive

dash, he always seemed to wear the number 4. Orr was more than the blond kid with a big smile and rock-solid build. He was a hockey hero every kid wanted to emulate.

One year the *The Boston Globe* held a poll to select the best athlete in the city's history. Ted Williams could have won. Or Bob Cousy or Carl Yazstremski or Bill Russell. But they didn't. Bobby Orr did.

Third, Orr rocked the hockey establishment. In 1963, Orr's father, Doug, heard lawyer Alan Eagleson make a speech at an award ceremony for Bobby's baseball team. Doug was impressed. He asked Eagleson to represent his boy. Bruins general manager Hap Emms was stunned when the Orrs told him that Bobby had a lawyer—player representation was new to the NHL. At that time, the average NHL rookie salary was $8,000. On September 3, 1966, Orr signed a two-year deal, including bonuses, for about $150,000. By the standards of the time, Orr had hit the jackpot. This led Eagleson to form the first successful players' union. Along with the advent of the World Hockey Association, the stage was set for the average NHL salary to jump from $15,000 to $55,000 during the next seven years.

Orr later had an ugly falling out with the Bruins and Eagleson, and ended his career with Chicago.

Fourth, Orr's knees ruined his career. Both knees were bad, but the left was worse for a longer period. In all, Orr underwent a half-dozen operations. His left-knee problems started in 1967–68, when he was trying to get away from Toronto's Marcel Pronovost. His second operation came after he got caught in a rut in the ice in LA. He had surgery again in June 1972 after he was injured playing against Detroit.

The problems never ended. He sat out a full season after his sixth operation. He tried a comeback in Chicago. It lasted 6 games. He retired November 1, 1978, at the tender age of thirty.

The Bruins' Bobby Orr redefined the position of defense and won NHL scoring titles in the process. But in the end, something went bad and Number 4 ended up in a Chicago Black Hawks uniform.

DENIS POTVIN

New York Rangers fans despised him. And virtually all his life, he was compared with Bobby Orr. But if any defenseman was ever prepared to handle the emotional weight of both Rangers fan wrath and Orr's giant shadow, it was Denis Potvin.

He could be controversial. He could be arrogant. His own teammates sometimes didn't get along with him. But he also could be personable and agreeable. He was dead honest. At times, his confidence crossed the line to cockiness.

He was like baseball's Reggie Jackson. He had some hot dog in him, but he rose to greatness when it mattered. He seemed to sense—better than many in the game—the importance of crucial moments.

Where Potvin should be placed all-time among defensemen can be debated. But nobody can deny there were great expectations from the beginning. He started playing major junior hockey in his hometown of Ottawa at fourteen, going against players five and six years older. He was the number one pick in the 1973 draft. Potvin didn't walk meekly into his first NHL camp. He strutted. He seemed to know that great Islander teams would be built around him. Coach Al Arbour actually came out and acknowledged it at one point. Potvin won the Calder Trophy as Rookie of the Year and kept improving until he scored 101 points in 1979. Then he led the Islanders to four Stanley Cups in a row.

When Denis Potvin retired, he was the highest scoring defenseman of all time with 310 goals, 742 assists, and 1,052 points. Paul Coffey, whose offensive skills and unparalleled skating speed were used for one-way offensive play, and Raymond Bourque have since passed him. But Potvin was never strictly about numbers anyway.

On the great New York Islanders team it was Mike Bossy who forever seemed to be judged by his statistics. But it was Potvin who became the essence of the team itself.

Denis could run and gun. He had a hard, wicked shot from the point. He could lead a rush like few before or after him. And he could quarterback a power play with a deft touch and unflappable cool.

Denis could be as wicked as anyone. He was a hard hitter. He was notorious for his death check, standing up an attacker at the blue line with a hit that could ruin knees. In 1979, he ended Ulf Nilsson's career. Rangers fans never forgot. Potvin broke Bengt Gustafsson's leg in 1986 with another devastating check.

At 205 pounds (93kg), Potvin was the complete package. He knew it. He wasn't afraid to tell people. But to the end, Potvin recognized that he wasn't a hero like Wayne Gretzky, Maurice Richard, or Bobby Orr. In other towns, he was labeled the villain. On Long Island, where he led the Islanders to four Stanley Cup champi-

onships, folks knew better. Three times he won the Norris Trophy as outstanding defenseman. Five times Potvin was a first-team All-Star.

He was a much better defensive player than Coffey. Fiercer, too. He remained healthier than Brad Park through his career. He had a little more offensive flair than Larry Robinson. And he lasted longer than Orr, who was hindered by knee problems.

But this didn't mean Potvin escaped the grind of professional hockey. He needed surgery to fix ligament damage in his thumb; he missed several weeks with a badly broken toe; and he had his share of groin pulls. But he kept on rolling along until he was thirty-four and retired on his own terms after the 1987–88 season. He was never traded, and some fans even wanted him to play another season or two.

Denis Potvin had to endure the terrible weight of being called "The Next Bobby Orr." Potvin never seemed to mind. He had the ego, talent, and competitive nature to handle it all.

MAURICE RICHARD

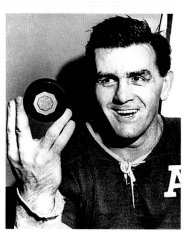

He had the most terrifying eyes in the history of hockey. They were two black chunks of charcoal ready to ignite at a second's notice. Indeed, the eyes were the fuse that lit the Rocket.

Maurice Richard, the idol of Montreal Canadiens fans for nearly two decades, wasn't the greatest player who ever lived. He was the greatest clutch goal scorer.

Consider the following theoretical question: "Big game in the sky. Tied 2–2 in second overtime. All the greatest players ever are suited up. Who scores the goal?"

The answer: the Rocket. Without a doubt.

He was the greatest opportunist hockey ever has seen.

He is the only man to score 6 playoff overtime goals in his career. Nobody else has scored 5.

Richard's 7 playoff hat tricks have been surpassed only by Wayne Gretzky, with 8. And the Great One has played 50 more playoff games than Richard.

Richard's 543 regular season goals stood as the NHL's career achievement until Gordie Howe broke the record in the early 1960s. He was the first man ever to score 50 goals in 50 games.

But Richard meant much more than numbers to French-Canadian fans. His passion and leadership in the face of great pressure made him a god in Montreal.

Interestingly enough, the man who became famous for possessing an iron will in an iron body was feared to be far too brittle in his youth. Growing up in Montreal, Maurice Richard spent many a night at Lafontaine Park and was a big-time scorer in the city's Park League. But he broke an ankle and fractured a wrist as an amateur. After making it to the Canadiens in 1942, he broke his ankle again. There was even some talk of releasing him because he seemed to be injury-prone. But visionary Montreal coach Dick Irvin wouldn't give up on

Richard, and Richard never gave up on his dream of achieving greatness.

Richard had a wicked temper—witness the unfortunate 1955 incident in which he attacked Boston's Hal Laycoe with his stick. Laycoe had high-sticked Richard, cutting him deeply enough to require several stitches. Richard went wild, attacking the Bruin with his stick and even punching referee Clint Thompson. NHL President Clarence Campbell suspended Richard for the rest of the season, leading to the infamous Richard Riot by fans in Montreal. How much did the Montreal fans love Rocket? They even booed his teammate Boom Boom Geoffrion for winning the scoring title in Rocket's absence.

Richard retired in 1960 after the Canadiens surged to their fifth successive Stanley Cup. He was the game's grand old man by that point. And there were oh so many memories of Stanley Cup glory. Like the semifinal game against Toronto in 1944 when the Canadiens won 5–1 and Richard scored all 5 goals. He scored 12 goals in 9 playoff games that spring. He was part of the Punch Line with Toe Blake and Elmer Lach in the 1940s. Later, Blake was his coach.

In April 1952 came another Richard classic in Game Seven of the semifinals against Boston. In the second period, Richard was crunched by Leo Labine and needed six stitches over his left eye. He didn't play for the rest of the second period and most of the third. He seemed dazed. With four minutes left, he finally got up off the Montreal bench and went onto the ice. Within seconds, he had skated through the entire Bruins team to score the winner. Richard later acknowledged that he was dizzy when he got the puck and didn't know if he was going toward his net or Boston's. The result, however, was captured for posterity in one of hockey's great photographs. With blood dripping down his face, Richard is seen shaking hands with Bruins goalie Jim Henry. Richard is steely-eyed. Henry is practically bowing in homage.

Opposite: Richard holds the puck with which he scored goal number 400, in 1954. Left: His most inspiring moment might have been the 1952 semifinals, when, half-conscious from a wicked Leo Labine check, the Rocket came off the bench to score the series clincher.

TERRY SAWCHUK

Emile Francis, who was general manager of the New York Rangers at the time, said one of the worst moments of his life was going down to the morgue in Manhattan to identify the body of Terry Sawchuk.

"There he was," Francis said, "the greatest goalie who ever lived, in a body bag that looked like one of those things you put hockey equipment in."

Thus ended the story of a great goalie and a troubled man. He died May 31, 1970, of a pulmonary embolism. The full story of what caused Sawchuk's death may never be known, but he had been out with Rangers teammate Ron Stewart, drinking was involved, and there was a fight—perhaps only drunken roughhousing. It ended up with Sawchuk getting nearly impaled on a barbecue spit.

Sawchuk was a brilliant goalie. Many contend he was the best. But he had a dark side. An incredible string of injuries and frayed nerves seemed to eat away at him.

It started when he was twelve. Growing up in Winnipeg, Sawchuk was warned by his parents not to play football. He did anyway and badly injured his right arm. Afraid of his parents' reaction, he said nothing. Eventually, his mom saw a huge lump in his arm. Sawchuk's elbow had been permanently dislocated and one arm was shorter than the other for the rest of his life.

When he was eighteen, he almost lost an eye from a skate cut. During his career, he also severed his hand tendons; fractured the instep of his foot; suffered a severe case of mononucleosis that caused a brief retirement from the Boston Bruins; fractured ribs and punctured a lung in a 1954 car accident; ruptured a disc; ruptured his appendix; and took more than four hundred stitches to his face.

Because of back problems, he walked around for years with a stoop. One year, weighing in at a chubby 230 pounds (104.4kg), he was ordered to trim down. He dropped 40 pounds (18.1kg), had trouble stopping the weight loss, and never put it back on. He became gaunt. Sawchuk used to say he spent every summer in the hospital. He wasn't stretching the truth by much.

Despite all this trauma, Sawchuk was a success from the start. He was Rookie of the Year in two minor leagues. When Detroit completed a highly controversial trade, moving Harry Lumley to make room for Sawchuk, the young sensation won the NHL Calder Trophy with an astonishing rookie season. He played all 70 games, and had 11 shutouts and a 1.99 goals-against average. Sawchuk won the Vezina Trophy as the goalie with the best average in 1952, 1953, and 1955. During the extraordinary five-year run that opened his NHL career, he had a 1.98 average and amassed 56 shutouts. In 1952, Sawchuk allowed only 5 goals in 9 games and had 4 shutouts to lead Detroit to the Stanley Cup.

Difficulties aside, Sawchuk was able to post 103 career shutouts, a record that may never be matched. He also contributed to the evolution of goaltending. He introduced the crouch, which allows goalies to better follow loose pucks and see through screens. Until that time, goalies stood up straight and bent slightly at the knees. The wisecrackers said Sawchuk looked like a gorilla.

Eventually, just as the Red Wings had traded away Lumley for Sawchuk, they traded Sawchuk to Boston to make room for young hotshot Glenn Hall. Sawchuk's family remained in Detroit. He was miserable. He came down with a severe case of mononucleosis and retired, deemed a quitter by some members of the Boston media who were unaware of his illness.

Sawchuk agreed to return to hockey when Detroit's Jack Adams talked the Bruins into allowing Detroit to reacquire his rights. Sawchuk played for the Wings for seven years in his second stint. Detroit, figuring he was all washed up at thirty-five, left Sawchuk off its protected list. Toronto claimed him and paired him with John Bower, forty-one. The old-timers combined to win the Vezina Trophy. And after returning from a back operation, Sawchuk led the Maple Leafs over Montreal for the 1967 Stanley Cup. He called it his greatest thrill.

Later, Sawchuk moved on to Los Angeles, to Detroit a third time, and finally to New York, where a twenty-year-old NHL career and a forty-year-old man met an inglorious ending.

Terry Sawchuk was a nervous, sometimes disagreeable fellow. But he overcame a medical book full of injuries and was arguably the greatest goalie who ever lived. His 103 career shutouts is one heck of an argument on his behalf.

Above: Eddie Shore and the Bruins took the Cup in 1929. The best defensive player of the NHL's formative decades, Shore has come to epitomize toughness, sheer determination, and the ability to star despite terrible injury. Opposite, middle row, second from left: Shore in 1929.

EDDIE SHORE

Whenever the phrase "old-time hockey" is uttered in cold, dank rinks today, the knowledgeable fan will smile and say, "Eddie Shore." For Eddie Shore truly stands for old-time hockey.

He was rough and mean and courageous. If Howie Morenz was the flashiest offensive star of the NHL's formative years, Eddie Shore was the game's defensive rock.

He scored 105 NHL goals, a formidable total for a defenseman in an era when essentially all they did was guard the front of their goalie's net. Instead of dumping the puck out of his own end or chopping it over to wingers along the boards, Shore carried the puck himself and led rushes like no defenseman before him. About thirty years later, another Boston Bruins defenseman by the name of Bobby Orr would push puck-carrying to an art form.

But the 105 goals are not the numbers that tell Shore's story.

These are: 978 stitches were amassed all over his body. He suffered a broken nose on fourteen occasions. He broke his jaw five times. He had most of his teeth knocked out.

Born in 1902, Shore came from Fort Qu'Appelle, Saskatchewan, where his family owned a farm and Shore developed a passion for breaking wild horses. Life was hard, the winters cold and harsh. He drove cattle through snowdrifts. A horse rolled over and fell on his shoulder, making it hard for him to lift his arm for several years.

He didn't skate particularly well until he was a teenager and was initially cut from the Manitoba Agricultural College hockey team. Shore persisted and worked his way through the Pacific Coast League, playing for Regina, Edmonton, and Victoria. He earned the name the Edmonton Express—he was a freight train. When the NHL moved into the United States, Shore became pivotal in selling professional hockey to Boston.

From there, the Shore legend grew.

In Shore's first year, Bruins defenseman Billy Coutu, sensing Shore could take his job away, decided to test the kid. They came to wicked blows. Shore's ear was nearly torn off. In fact, the Bruins doctor wanted to amputate. Shore kept seeking another opinion until he found a doctor to reattach the dangling flesh.

Then on January 2, 1929, Shore missed the train headed for Montreal because of a Boston traffic jam. The Bruins were already short a defenseman because of an injury. Shore got a wealthy friend to provide him with a car and a chauffeur, but the driver, daunted by the prospect of navigating through a blizzard, gave up.

Shore drove the car through Vermont and on to Montreal himself. When the windows froze over, he pushed open the windshield and took the snow directly in the face. When the car slid into a deep ditch, Shore persuaded a farmer to use his horse to get the car back on the road. He arrived in Montreal, half-frozen and nearly delirious at 6 P.M.

He insisted on playing. And except for 1 penalty, he was on the ice the entire game. He scored the only goal in a 1–0 victory over the Maroons.

Shore won the Hart Trophy as the NHL's most valuable player in 1933, 1935, 1936, and 1938 and was named first-team All-Star seven times. Later he would settle in as owner of the Springfield team in the AHL, distinguishing himself as tough and frugal. He was old-time hockey.

THE GREATEST MOMENTS

What is the most unforgettable hockey moment?

It depends on your nationality. It depends on your age. It depends on your favorite team or player.

Ask a middle-aged fan in Toronto, and the answer undoubtedly is Paul Henderson scoring the dramatic goal to lift Canada over the Soviet Union in the 1972 Summit Series. Heck, it saved Canada's national pride.

Ask a fan in the United States, and the answer has got to be the 1980 Olympic gold medal victory at Lake Placid. What could be greater than Al Michaels asking us if we believe in miracles?

A devoted fan in Montreal can answer that. It has to be one of the Canadiens' twenty-four Stanley Cups or some remarkable performance involving Rocket Richard, Jean Beliveau, or Guy Lafleur.

The truth, of course, is there is no scoreboard to define the greatest, the worst, the most hilarious moment. Those moments exist only in the hearts and minds of hockey fans.

Edmonton Oilers fans enjoyed a decade full of highs in the 1980s, but none of them will forget the low of April 30, 1986, when defenseman Steve Smith attempted a clearing pass from behind his net and, instead, banked the puck off the back of goalie Grant Fuhr's leg and into his own net. The blunder, which came in the third period of Game Seven of the Smythe Division finals, cost the Oilers a third Stanley Cup in a row.

Bobby Orr, Ray Bourque, and Phil Esposito lit up Boston Garden for years. But Bruins fans will not forget the night the lights went out in Boston. On May 24, 1988, the puck was about to be dropped in the second period of Game Four of the Stanley Cup finals. The Garden went dark. And stayed dark. It turned out that a transformer had blown, but at the time it seemed like the end of the world. The night ended in a 3–3 tie. The game was replayed a few nights later in Edmonton, where the Oilers completed a sweep to the Stanley Cup in Game 4A.

Wayne Gretzky once called the New Jersey Devils a "Mickey Mouse" organization, but it was the entire NHL that looked dopey on May 7, 1988, at the Meadowlands. A few nights earlier, Devils coach Jim Schoenfeld had yelled at referee Don Koharski, "Have another doughnut, you fat pig!" The NHL suspended Schoenfeld. The Devils obtained a restraining order to block the suspension. But fearing for their safety, the scheduled officials refused to work Game Four of the semifinals. It finally started one hour late with two local amateur officials in ill-fitting yellow jerseys working the game. Nobody could find NHL President John Ziegler that night.

Fortunately, there have been thousands of brighter, better, funnier, more poignant, and generally unforgettable moments in the history of hockey.

Opposite: Mario Lemieux's back problems couldn't stop him from hoisting two Stanley Cups. Above: Toronto fans have not seen the Stanley Cup hoisted since Maple Leafs captain George Amstrong celebrated in 1967.

THE LONGEST JOURNEY TO DEFEAT

January 15, 1905

Ottawa's Frank McGee may have had only one eye on the Stanley Cup in 1905, but all of Canada was watching the 4,400-mile (7,040km) journey by the Dawson City Klondikers. The result was hockey legend.

In the early years of Stanley Cup competition, an opponent could simply issue a challenge, step right up, and take his best swings at the champ. The procedure was similar to boxing matches at old state fairs. Sometimes the matches were brilliant. Sometimes they were blowouts. In this case, however, the Klondikers' romantic trek from the Yukon captured the imagination of folks across Canada.

At the turn of the century, the Yukon was a mini version of California in the 1840s. The gold rush was on. Free-spirited adventurers and get-rich-quick schemers journeyed to one of the coldest places on earth to seek their fortune. It was left up to Colonel Joe Boyle, who had gotten lucky and struck it rich, to issue a challenge to the Ottawa Silver Seven for the prize set up by Lord Stanley of Preston in 1892.

The Klondikers had pulled together the $3,000 to get to Ottawa. And although more talented teams could not handle the Silver Seven's sometimes cruel physical play, these lean, rollicking Yukon prospectors weren't intimidated. The big problem was drumming up enough skilled players to seriously challenge the day's dominant team.

The Klondikers came up with goalie Albert Forrest, at seventeen the youngest player in Stanley Cup history. They gathered a group of nine rollicking lads who had crossed the continent from Quebec, Ontario, and Manitoba to get to the Yukon and who were now willing to travel back across the country to take on the Ottawa team. Along the way, as their twenty-day journey turned epic, Lorne Hanna of Brandon, Manitoba, signed on to play.

On December 19, 1904, the Klondikers left Dawson City by dogsled. They covered forty-six miles (73.6km) the first day, forty-one miles (65.6km) the second, and thirty-six miles (57.6km) the next. The temperature dropped to twenty degrees below zero (-28°C). Running or walking alongside their sleds, the players developed painful blisters. (It's a wonder they didn't develop frostbite!) The Klondikers missed the steamship from Skagway, near Juneau, Alaska, by only a few hours and were forced to wait at the dock for five days for another boat to Seattle. From Seattle, it was on to Vancouver and then across the continent by train. Everywhere the Klondikers traveled, they were greeted by cheering throngs.

The Klondikers finally arrived in Ottawa on January 12, 1905, only one day before the best-of-three series was set to begin. They asked the Silver Seven to postpone the series for a week to allow them to rest. Ottawa refused.

Maybe the Dawson City fellows were bitter about the scheduling. Maybe they were just crazy. For whatever reason, even after Ottawa won Game One handily, with a score of 9–2, one of the Klondikers foolishly remarked that McGee, the blind-in-one-eye Silver Seven star, didn't "look like much." McGee had scored only 1 goal. Aroused by the slight, in Game Two McGee rose to the challenge, scoring a Stanley Cup record 14 goals, including 8 in a row, for a 23–2 rout. "One-Eyed" Frank McGee, tragically killed during World War I at the battle of the Somme, had taught the Klondikers a lesson about toughness, and the longest road trip in Stanley Cup history ended in the worst beating in its annals.

And Forrest, the beleaguered goalie? He walked the final 350 miles (560km) from Pelly Crossing home to Dawson City alone.

The rollicking Dawson City Klondikers, photographed in Ottawa in 1905, journeyed more than four thousand miles (6,400km) from the Yukon for a Stanley Cup challenge. They lost, 23–2.

THE OLD MAN IN GOAL

April 7, 1928

Can you imagine today's coaches tossing off their Armani suits and Gucci loafers to play goal in the pressure cooker of the Stanley Cup playoffs? Not likely, eh? Yet this is precisely what Lester Patrick did in Game Two of the 1928 finals.

Patrick's New York Rangers were already facing a serious disadvantage. Because the circus was scheduled for Madison Square Garden, the Rangers were forced to play all 5 games against the Maroons at Montreal Forum.

But even dropping the opener, 2–0, did not prepare the Rangers for what would occur four minutes into the second period of Game Two. Nels Stewart, nicknamed Ole Poison for his deadly shot, unleashed a backhander that caught New York goalie Lorne Chabot in the left eye. The eyeball hemorrhaged. The crowd of twelve thousand grew quiet as he was carried off the ice on a stretcher. Chabot would not play again in the series.

Today, a backup goalie could step in and write an inspiring script. But this was 1928 and teams carried only one goalie. Coach Lester Patrick had ten minutes to find a replacement. Ottawa goalie Alex Connell was in the stands as a spectator. The Rangers thought they were in luck. But Eddie Gerard, the Maroons manager, refused to grant him permission to play. Gerard uttered these defiant words: "Suckers were born yesterday and you're talking to the wrong man."

The Rangers turned to Hughie McCormick, a minor leaguer, also in attendance. But again Gerard refused, citing an NHL rule that if a team needed to replace its goaltender, the substitute must be under contract to that team. Patrick had a long face as he returned to the locker room to tell his boys one of them would be forced to play goal. Frank Boucher, Patrick's most gifted player, suggested Patrick put on the pads. "I'm too old," Patrick, forty-four, protested.

Years earlier, Patrick had been an excellent defenseman. And because goalies used to serve their own penalties, Patrick, on rare occasions, did fill in at goal. But this was much, much different. His players pushed him into goaltending equipment he knew nothing about. Patrick was trembling. To give him confidence, his players put easy shots on him in warmups.

But the man nicknamed The Silver Fox soon recovered his nerve. Although his players did an outstanding job keeping the Maroons from swarming the old man, Patrick did stop 18 shots. Soon Patrick was shouting in mock seriousness to his players to allow the Maroons to shoot on him.

The Rangers clung to a 1–0 lead until the closing six minutes, when Stewart struck again. Ole Poison didn't hit Patrick in the eye, but he tied the game. Then Boucher, the man who had pushed his coach to play goal, stole the puck, broke in alone, and scored the winner at 7:05 of overtime.

Patrick's players carried him off the ice, their leader shedding tears of elation. The Montreal fans, despite their team's loss, rose to give Patrick a tremendous ovation. The Silver Fox was too smart to stage an encore. The Rangers brought in Joe Miller, who played for the New York Americans, to finish the series. Miller allowed only 3 goals in 3 games. In the last game, Miller fell on a stick and suffered two black eyes and a badly cut nose. This time, Patrick stayed behind the bench. Miller finished the game and the Rangers took the Stanley Cup.

Rangers coach Lester Patrick stepped out of street clothes and into immortality as he replaced injured goalie Lorne Chabot and beat the Maroons in Game Two of the 1928 Stanley Cup finals.

Above: A 1933 benefit for Ace Bailey led to the formation of the NHL All-Star Game and gave the men a chance to end their differences. Opposite: Bailey is carried off the ice by his teammates. Bailey survived the brutal attack by Boston's Eddie Shore, but Bailey never played again.

HOCKEY'S WORST MOMENT

December 12, 1933

There is no escaping the argument. Hockey can be a violent, cruel game. Entanglements over the decades have involved players, coaches, and officials, and have even spilled into the stands to include fans. But perhaps the most violent moment in NHL history was over quickly. It involved one brutal hit and one brutal retaliation.

Yet because of the stature of the players involved and the near-fatal injury Toronto's Ace Bailey sustained, the moment lives in hockey infamy. The story is not all bad. The vicious attack resulted in the formation of the NHL All-Star Game for the benefit of charities. The first benefit was for Bailey himself.

Boston Bruins defenseman Eddie Shore was the best defenseman in the pre–War World II NHL. He was fierce. He was belligerent. He was known for both his competitive drive and his savage hits. Ironically, Shore had tried to play with a more gentlemanly flavor earlier in the 1932–33 season. This restraint only served to frustrate the beast within Shore. The frustration broke out on December 12, 1933.

While the Leafs were killing off a two-man power play, defenseman King Clancy, who had made a career of agitating Shore, lined Eddie up and sent him sprawling with a clean body check. Clancy weighed only 150 pounds (67.5kg), but he was wiry. Shore landed on his knees and slid to the boards. He was seething.

Shore later said he was knocked daffy. At any rate, Shore burst up full speed and piled into Bailey, who flew into the air and crashed head-first into the ice. The thud was sickening. Bailey's head was contorted at a strange angle. Some have argued that Shore, dazed, mistook Bailey for Clancy. Others think Shore was embarrassed that a lightweight like Clancy crushed him.

Red Horner rushed to Bailey, kneeling over his fallen teammate. Horner climbed to his feet and said, "Why did you do that, Eddie?" Shore said nothing. He only smiled. Horner went bonkers. He landed a vicious right uppercut to Shore's chin. Shore fell backward, hitting his head on the ice. Blood was everywhere.

In a flash, the incident was over. Shore turned out to be okay, but Bailey's life was in danger. He was rushed to the hospital in critical condition with a double skull fracture. Surgeons in Boston performed two operations on Bailey. He was watched by nurses day and night. Leafs owner Conn Smythe even made arrangements for Bailey's body to be taken back to Toronto. After ten terrible days, it was clear Bailey would live, but he would never play hockey again.

While Shore served a 16-game suspension and went for a vacation in Bermuda, Smythe argued that the Bruins should indemnify his team for his losses. A compromise was reached, and it led to the first NHL All-Star Game. On February 14, 1934, the Leafs and the NHL All-Stars played for the benefit of an Ace Bailey Fund. The affair raised more than $20,000. But the Leafs' 7–3 victory was overshadowed by a dramatic pregame moment. With the teams lined up along the blue lines, Bailey walked slowly to center ice. He wore eyeglasses. He looked older than his years. Fans held their breath. Tension filled the arena. What would happen? Suddenly, Shore skated from his spot in the All-Star lineup and extended his hand. Bailey grasped it and the two stars embraced. Folks who attended the game said Maple Leaf Gardens trembled that night.

THE LONGEST GAME

March 25, 1936

To love hockey is to love sudden-death overtime in the Stanley Cup playoffs. One may argue with validity that the penalty shot is the single most exciting moment in this sport. But the penalty shot is an individual duel between shooter and goalie. Overtime is a tightrope walk for everybody involved. The most important game of any season can end in a split second. One mistake can ruin careers. One goal can make legends. Overtime games can drag on unmercifully through a humid spring night and suddenly—bang—it's in the net and the building erupts as if an earthquake has hit.

Maurice Richard is the playoff career legend with 6 overtime goals. For a single series, nobody can match Boston's Mel "Sudden Death" Hill. He scored only 89 goals in his career, but in 1939 Hill went from the anonymous to the heroic in a semifinal series against the Rangers. Hill scored 3 overtime winners, including the third one in overtime in a decisive Game Seven.

There have been so many thrilling overtimes since, including the longest overtime in Cup finals history in 1990 when Petr Klima hopped off the bench after a two-hour rest. Having not played since the third period of regulation, Klima scored at 15:13 of the third overtime period to win Game One.

But whenever discussion turns to great overtime moments, inevitably the focus falls on a rookie named Mud. That's short for Bruneteau's first name, Modere. During the 1930s, games were low-scoring and overtime was common. But this playoff semifinal game between Detroit and the Montreal Maroons, which started at 8:35 P.M. on March 24, would prove to be the longest hockey game in history.

The first period was scoreless. The second period? Scoreless. The third period? You guessed it. Scoreless. The game moved into overtime. The first overtime yielded no goals. Neither did the second, the third, or the fourth. Near the end of the fifth overtime, Detroit's Herb Lewis, set up by Martin Barry, broke in and shot on Montreal goalie Lorne Chabot. The puck struck the goal post. The Forum crowd uttered a collective groan.

NHL President Frank Calder was faced with a dilemma. These teams looked as if they might play until Judgment Day without a winner. Oddly, he rejected the idea of resuming the game the following night. Calder was willing to allow a coin flip to decide the winner. That offer was refused.

When the teams remained locked in a scoreless game through 4:46 of the sixth overtime, Detroit and the Maroons broke the longest-game mark set three years earlier by Toronto and Boston. The decisive moment finally arrived with 3:30 remaining in the sixth overtime—or 3:30 short of three complete regulation games. Red Wings goalie Norm Smith kicked out his ninetieth save, leading to a man-advantage break for the Wings.

It was 2:25 A.M. Hec Kilrea and Bruneteau closed on the able Lionel Conacher. Conacher lost his skating edge on an ice surface that had deteriorated into poor condition from this seemingly endless game. Bruneteau had scored only 2 goals all season, but he made no mistake on this play. He deked Chabot and drove in the goal. An incredible five hours and fifty-one minutes after this game had started, the only goal was scored. The Red Wings went on to win the Stanley Cup.

The guy's name was Mud. But after Modere "Mud" Bruneteau scored in the sixth overtime to lift the Montreal Maroons over Detroit in the 1936 NHL semifinals, everybody was a day older.

BARILKO'S FINAL GOAL

April 21, 1951

The year was 1951. It was a time of fierce rivalries and heart-stopping finishes. Later that autumn, baseball player Bobby Thomson would launch the "shot heard 'round the world" at the Polo Grounds in New York. Thomson would be lionized throughout America for dramatically lifting his Giants over the Brooklyn Dodgers to the National League pennant. A parallel story emerged north of the border. Tragically, it ended in a crash heard nowhere in the world.

For four months, Toronto Maple Leafs defenseman Bill Barilko was the hero of English-speaking Canada and the toast of the hockey world. It was not a throne he had been destined to inherit. He was not a devastating goal scorer. He was not a glitzy stickhandler. Barilko was a rock-hard defenseman with a penchant for wicked body checks. The Montreal Canadiens' Elmer Lach called Barilko the hardest hitter in hockey. His hips were lethal. Barilko was annually among the league leaders in penalty minutes.

In Game One of the Stanley Cup finals, Barilko sprawled to block what appeared to be a sure winning goal for Maurice Richard of the Montreal Canadiens in the closing minutes of regulation. The Leafs went on to win that game.

But on April 21, Barilko devastated the Montreal Canadiens and their legions of fans in a most unusual manner. He scored the sudden-death overtime goal that beat the Canadiens to give the Maple Leafs their fourth Stanley Cup in five years.

The Canadiens trailed the series 3 games to 1 but were leading Game Five 2–1 with sixty seconds remaining at Maple Leaf Gardens.

Toronto coach Joe Primeau pulled his goalie and sent Max Bentley onto the ice as an extra attacker. Bentley and Teeder Kennedy combined to send Tod Sloan rushing in on the net, and he beat Canadiens goalie Gerry McNeil with only thirty-two seconds left to tie the game.

This set the stage for Barilko. At 2:53 of overtime, the bushy blond-haired kid out of northern Ontario stepped up to play his unforgettable role in hockey history. He had scored neither a goal nor an assist the entire series. But taking a pass from Howie Meeker as he sliced over the Canadiens' blue line, Barilko cut in on McNeil. He put so much effort into his shot that he flung himself into the air. When he landed, the puck was in the net. The Stanley Cup belonged to the Maple Leafs.

Although Toronto had won 4 of the 5 games, these numbers simply cannot do justice to the brilliance of that competition. It was the only time in NHL history that every single game in a playoff series went into overtime.

Barilko returned to his hometown of Timmins, Ontario, a hero. Later that summer, he decided to get away for some relaxation in the northern bush country and do some fishing with his friend Dr. Henry Hudson, a local dentist. On August 26, the two took off in Hudson's plane for the final leg of the trip from Seal River back to Timmins. The plane went down in the wilderness. Northern Ontario is a vast area of untamed woods and a maze of lakes. A search produced nothing, although eleven years later, remains of the wreckage were believed to have been found. It took that long—until 1962—for the Toronto Maple Leafs to win another Stanley Cup.

Toronto's Bill Barilko became a hero throughout English-speaking Canada when he scored the Stanley Cup–winning goal in 1951. Barilko never scored again. He was lost in a plane crash that summer during a fishing trip.

THE FASTEST HAT TRICK

March 23, 1952

This night should have been a one-way ticket to the land of the eminently forgettable. The Chicago Black Hawks were destined for last place in the NHL. The New York Rangers were destined for next-to-last. It was the last game of the season. Dreams of playoffs were long dead. Only 3,254 fans bothered to show up at Madison Square Garden. Referee George Gravel didn't bother calling a penalty all night.

But out of nowhere, the forgettable became the unforgettable. The hockey gods seemed to slip down and touch Chicago's Bill Mosienko. Suddenly, he wore the wings of Mercury. Unexpectedly, he had a magic wand. Most NHL players long for one hat trick in their career. To score 3 goals in one period is extremely rare. To score 3 goals in twenty-one seconds was unheard of. No team, in fact, had ever scored 3 goals in twenty-one seconds.

It didn't hurt that the Rangers' number one goalie, Chuck Rayner, was out with an injury. It didn't hurt that Rayner's backup, Emile "the Cat" Francis, had been assigned to Cincinnati of the American Hockey League to help its playoff drive, leaving Lorne Anderson, who had played only 2 NHL games, in goal. Anderson was the goalie for the New York Rovers, the Rangers' farm team in the Eastern Hockey League. But he was performing just fine through the early minutes of the third period. The Rangers held a commanding 6–2 lead.

Mosienko's center, Gus Bodnar, found Mosienko in flight through the neutral zone. Mosienko beat defenseman Hy Buller. Buller was second-team NHL All-Star that year. He was no slouch, but he was trying to play hurt. And although Mosienko was thirty years old, he was still swift. Mosienko got around Buller and beat Anderson with a low wrist shot to the goalie's right at 6:09 of the third. Mosienko followed the puck into the net to retrieve it. In those days, 30 goals in a season was a nice trick. It was number 29 for Mosienko, and he figured this was as close as he'd get.

Only eleven seconds later, Mosienko struck again. Bodnar won the ensuing face-off at center ice and found Mosienko in full stride. He zipped past Buller again. Again he beat Anderson to the glove side. Mosienko headed back into the net to retrieve the puck for goal number 30.

Bodnar won another center ice draw, but this time he passed the puck to George Gee on the left wing. Mosienko kept pace and suddenly burst for the net. Gee saw him and made a perfect pass. By this point Anderson thought he had Mosiensko figured out. He guessed Mosienko would go low on the glove side one final time. Instead, Mosienko pulled him out of the goal and scored into the other side of the goal. Mosienko had no idea he had made NHL history and didn't retrieve this puck. Teammate Jimmy Peters, knowing better, grabbed the puck—and it's in the Hockey Hall of Fame today.

Mosienko, incredibly, had a chance to score a fourth goal seconds later, but his shot just missed the post. Coach Ebbie Goodfellow, showing a wry sense of humor, yelled for Mosienko to get off the ice because he was in a slump.

Jean Bealiveau scored 3 goals in forty-four seconds in 1955, but in more than thirty years that's as close as anybody has ever come to Mosienko's record. Ed Westfall, John Bucyk, and Ted Green did combine to give the Bruins 3 goals in twenty seconds in 1970. And poor Lorne Anderson? The Rangers lost 7–6 and he never played another game in the NHL.

For twenty-one seconds one night in 1952, Chicago's Bill Mosienko could do no wrong and Rangers goalie Lorne Anderson could do nothing right. Mosienko's hat trick rewrote the record books.

THE RICHARD RIOT

St. Patrick's Day, 1955

When it comes to passion and fervor, nobody can match the Montreal fans who live and die with Les Habitants. The Montreal Canadiens aren't a sports franchise. They are a religion.

And the high priest for nearly two decades was Maurice "Rocket" Richard. All the love and adulation heaped on Richard, however, boiled over into the hottest, ugliest mess in hockey history on St. Patrick's Day, 1955. It became known as the Richard Riot, and the 1954–55 NHL season hung on its resolution.

It's not that Richard didn't end up getting what he deserved. He did. But fairness and justice were not on Canadiens' fans minds that March. The insatiable demand for another Stanley Cup—something these fans feel is their divine right—was burning in their hearts.

Richard was as well known for his volatile temper as he was for his explosive scoring touch. And Richard already had endured a number of run-ins with NHL President Clarence Campbell when things got hot again on March 13.

The Bruins' bespectacled Hal Laycoe high-sticked Richard on the head, giving him a cut that required eight stitches. Laycoe got a delayed penalty. Richard went berserk. When play stopped, Richard showed the referee where he had been cut. Suddenly, he charged Laycoe and swung his stick wildly. He hit Laycoe.

Twice Richard was pulled back by officials and forced to relinquish his stick. Twice Richard broke away, picked up another stick from the ice, and charged Laycoe. Linesman Cliff Thompson finally wrestled the menacing bull to the ice. But when Richard climbed back on his skates, he cuffed Thompson in the face.

Campbell was irate. He didn't care that the Detroit Red Wings and the Canadiens were locked in a fierce battle for first place. He didn't

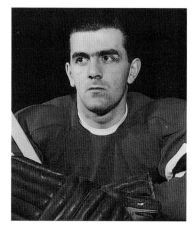

care that Richard and teammates Bernie Geoffrion and Jean Beliveau were locked in a three-way race for the scoring title. Campbell suspended Richard for the rest of the season, including the playoffs.

Montreal fans, sensing doom, reacted with fury. Campbell refused to be intimidated and, resolute, positioned himself in his accustomed Forum seat for the key Detroit-Montreal match on March 17.

The Red Wings grabbed a 4–1 lead; then the trouble started. Campbell was pelted by popcorn, programs, peanuts, and rotten eggs. One fan acted as if he was going to shake Campbell's hand and, instead, smacked him. As Montreal police and Forum security closed in, a canister of tear gas was thrown near Campbell's seat. Montreal Fire Marshal Armand Pare cleared the building. Campbell declared Detroit the winner by forfeit.

Trouble continued outside the Forum. An angry mob looted stores, smashed windows, and damaged autos. Sixty people were arrested. There were fears that the ugly scene would be repeated, and Campbell was advised by Mayor Jean Drapeau to stay away from the Forum. Richard, showing great dignity, held a news conference the following day and broadcast an appeal for order over the radio. He told his fans he would accept his punishment and come back next year to help win the Stanley Cup. This move cooled the tensions.

With Richard out of the picture, Detroit finished first in the regular season and won the Stanley Cup in 1955. And although Richard remained upset for years that Campbell wouldn't allow him to play in the 1955 playoffs, he did better than keep his promise to win the Stanley Cup the following year. Richard and the Canadiens won a record five Cups in a row.

Maurice "Rocket" Richard's eyes burned with desire. But the passion the Montreal great inspired in his fans poured over into an ugly riot in 1955. When the smoke cleared, the area near the Montreal Forum was trashed and the Montreal Canadiens had forfeited the game to Detroit.

PLANTE COVERS HIS FACE

November 1, 1959

With pucks flashing past in excess of one hundred miles per hour (160kph), the notion of a bare-faced goalie almost seems absurd today. Why would anyone allow his face to go unprotected against the best shooters in hockey?

Goalie masks have undergone a fascinating transformation in the past thirty-five years, evolving from the primitive to the highly polished. And as a result, goalies no longer risk losing their sight or having their brains scrambled.

Incredibly, goalies still weren't wearing masks late in the Eisenhower administration even as the space age was getting under way. The no-mask era ended when the hockey world, filled with equal parts doubt and machismo, bowed before Jacques Plante, the great goalie of the Montreal Canadiens.

Plante was a quirky fellow. Management and fans were often down on him, second-guessing his seemingly endless string of injuries and asthma attacks. He was a loner who preferred books and painting to parties. He even knitted his own undershirts if he couldn't find the kind he wanted in the store.

Plante had suffered more than two hundred facial stitches in his career. He had sustained two broken cheekbones, four broken noses, and a fractured skull. For months, he had been toying with the idea of wearing a mask in games. It was not a novel thought. Clint Benedict had worn a mask briefly in 1929 before giving up on it. Other goalies practiced with wire masks, similar to those of baseball catchers. But those masks were clumsy and limited the goalies' vision.

During the 1958 playoffs, a shot cut Plante on the forehead. Bill Burchmore of Fibreglas Canada had seen the game and wrote a letter to Plante promoting the idea of a lightweight, tight-fitting mask

to be molded to the goaltender's face. Plante went for it.

He wore the mask in the preseason and was greeted with criticism. He was even accused of losing his nerve. Montreal coach Toe Blake was convinced that Plante would lose sight of the fast-moving puck. The idea was put on hold for more than a month.

On November 1, 1959, Andy Bathgate of the New York Rangers unleashed a backhander from the side of the net. Screened by a maze of players, Plante didn't see it coming and was struck in the face. The puck sliced the side of his nose; it took seven stitches to close the deep gash. Blood splashed his white jersey.

A test of wills quickly developed. Plante refused to go back into the game unless he could wear his mask. Since the home team was designated to provide a backup goalie (teams were not yet carrying backups) and the game was in Madison Square Garden, a fellow named Joe Schaefer, pudgy and nearly forty, was Blake's only option. Blake relented. Plante could wear his mask.

Plante played splendidly, beating the Rangers, 3–1. In fact, he went on to win 11 games in a row. Canadiens manager Frank Selke was still a doubter. He sent Plante to eye doctors for vision checks with and without the mask. Plante would not relent. The Bruins' Don Simmons became the second goalie to go to a mask and promptly posted 2 shutouts. Rangers manager Muzz Patrick was convinced. He made goalie masks compulsory for his minor leaguers. Still, not everybody was convinced. Terry Sawchuk didn't don a mask until three years later. And even as hockey entered the 1970s, Gump Worsley, Joe Daley, and Andy Brown continued to go barefaced. But they were dinosaurs bent on extinction. Plante, through his persistence, had begun an irreversible trend.

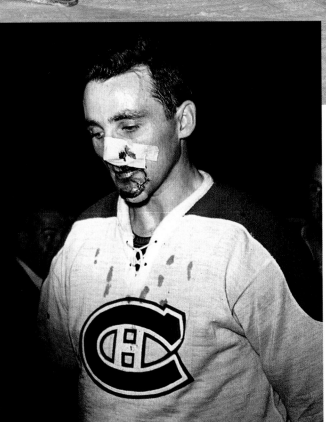

A 25-foot (7.5m) backhander by the Rangers' Andy Bathgate opened a gash on Jacques Plante's nose. Maybe it was machismo. Maybe those who ran hockey were convinced masks impaired vision. Until Montreal's Jacques Plante, bleeding badly, refused to play without facial protection in 1959, goalie masks were seen as a sign of weakness.

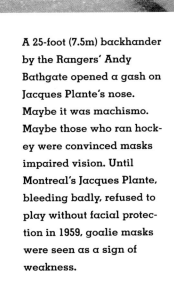

HOWE CATCHES THE ROCKET

November 10, 1963

For decades, the most famous statistic in all of sports was 714. That's how many home runs Babe Ruth hit in his baseball career. It was a numerical monument supposedly built to stand forever. Hank Aaron tore it down with 715 in April 1974.

Although less well known in the United States, the number 544 evoked similar feelings in the hearts of Montreal's fervent fans. That's how many goals Rocket Richard scored in his 978-game career, which ended after the Canadiens captured their fifth successive Stanley Cup in 1960.

But hockey fans in Montreal should have taken off those bleu, blanc, et rouge glasses that altered their objectivity. There was a strapping right winger from Floral, Saskatchewan, who was destined to burst past the Rocket's red glare. Gordie Howe, Mr. Hockey, would play parts of five decades in the NHL and his record of 801 goals would stand until Wayne Gretzky surpassed him in 1994.

But the time was the early 1960s. Nobody had ever scored 55 goals in one season, let alone the 92 that Gretzky would amass two decades later. And Howe, who had absorbed a terrific beating over the years, had dropped to 32 goals in 1958–59, 28 in 1959–60, and 23 in 1960–61. Nobody at that point could imagine that Howe's career would last until 1980 with the Hartford Whalers. In 1960, there was actually talk of Howe being pushed back to a more defensive line for the twilight of his career. Howe had other ideas. In 1961–62, he scored 33 goals, second only to Bobby Hull. In 1962–63, he scored 38.

Suddenly, Howe could see the Rocket's taillights. And, oh, those Canadiens fans didn't like it one bit. On October 27, 1963, the Red Wings and Canadiens collided. Montreal coach Toe Blake used a fasci-

nating ploy. He made sure Richard's brother, Henri, was on the ice every time Howe was. Blake was playing mind games. He buttressed this maneuver by using winger Gilles Tremblay to shadow Gordie's every move. It almost worked. Howe generated just 2 shots on goal all night. But 1 was a third-period goal for number 544. In a touching moment of sportsmanship that followed, gentleman Jean Beliveau, captain of the Canadiens, took off his glove and shook Howe's hand.

Howe and the Red Wings immediately went into a slump. He didn't score a goal for 5 games. His nervous twitch got worse. Reporters tired of following Howe from city to city. But there would be an unforeseen benefit. The slump gave Howe the chance to snap Richard's record at the Detroit Olympia against the Canadiens.

The Olympia held 12,500 seats, but 15,027 people jammed the place to watch Howe's glorious moment. Again Blake used his shadowing strategy. The only difference was that Charlie Hodge was in goal instead of Gump Worsley. Howe was held off the scoreboard through the early part of the second period. It didn't look any better when Red Wing Alex Faulkner was nailed for a five-minute penalty for high-sticking. Howe went to the penalty kill. Billy McNeill gained control of the puck deep in his zone and Howe screamed at him to keep moving. He sliced into the offensive zone with Howe chasing. McNeill poked the puck to Howe and in one swift motion he scored what McNeill called "a perfect goal," number 545. The Olympia fans went wild.

Howe's number 600 would arrive on November 27, 1965. Number 700 came December 4, 1968, and Howe passed Babe Ruth on February 6, 1969. Before Howe had finished in 1980, he had 801 goals in the NHL and more than 1,000 total in his career.

Gordie Howe broke into the NHL in 1946. He played his last game in 1980. His list of records was long. But the Howe legend was certified on November 10, 1963, when he scored a shorthanded goal on Montreal's Charlie Hodge for his 545th goal to snap Maurice Richard's NHL record.

ORR DEFIES GRAVITY

Mother's Day, 1970

Few teams captured the hearts and imaginations of the people of an entire region like the Boston Bruins in the late 1960s and the early 1970s. For sports fans in New England—from New London, Connecticut, to Bangor, Maine—it was the golden age of the Bruins.

Phil Esposito owned the slot and seemed to score at will. Ken Hodge and Wayne Cashman were big, strong cornermen who seemed unstoppable on a line with Esposito. Gerry Cheevers gave new meaning to the words *clutch goaltending*. Derek Sanderson, a checking

demon and face-off wizard, was one of the best young centers in the game. The Turk had a big moustache and was an idol. There was no smoother performer on the wing than John Bucyk. Dallas Smith was a rock on defense. John McKenzie was the ultimate pest. The list went on. But nobody even tried to deny that Orr was the best player. He gave a new definition to what a defenseman could accomplish.

The big, bad Bruins were a rollicking bunch, often compared to the Gashouse Gang, the St. Louis Cardinals. They had zany personalities. And they were as close a group as any in hockey history. When, for

example, Phil Esposito was stuck in the hospital after knee surgery, several Bruins slipped into the hospital ward and wheeled him and his bed out of the place for some fun at Orr's restaurant a few blocks away. Twenty years later, every member of the Stanley Cup team showed up for a four-day reunion.

The big, bad Bruins were a big deal in Boston and beyond. And the whole joyous ride was captured in one photograph taken on Mother's Day 1970. It is a single moment, preserved in black and white, that unleashes a thousand memories. There is Bobby Orr flying through the Boston Garden air. He is three feet (0.9m) off the earth's surface, flying parallel to the ice. His arms are outstretched. His stick is pointing to the heavens, a lightning rod to the hockey gods. His mouth is open in awe of what he has accomplished. St. Louis Blues defenseman Noel Picard watches grimly. He is the man who had tripped Orr. But instead of Orr tumbling to the ice as Picard had intended, Orr took off for outer space. Blues goalie Glenn Hall is sprawled backward into the net, shattered. And in the background are hundreds of Boston Garden fans leaping to their feet in joy, their arms raised.

Hockey has a long, storied history in Massachusetts. But the Bruins had missed the playoffs every year from 1960 to 1967 and they had not won a Stanley Cup since 1941; the Stanley Cup-starved fans knew 1970 would be different. The Bruins outlasted the Rangers in a wicked 6-game series before stunning the powerful Chicago Black Hawks in a 4-game sweep. Then the Bruins swept the overmatched St. Louis Blues in the championship series.

Orr's overtime goal in Game Four put an exclamation point on the matter. He worked a give-and-go with Derek Sanderson and zipped in on Hall, and the rest is history. If Orr had failed, he would have left the Blues with a four-on-one break up-ice. Orr did not fail.

The Bruins did win a second Stanley Cup in 1972, but they probably should have won four titles. After smashing a frightening number of offensive records in 1971, Montreal Canadiens goalie Ken Dryden stymied the Bruins in a heroic playoff performance. And after 1972, injuries and defections to the rival World Hockey Association took their toll.

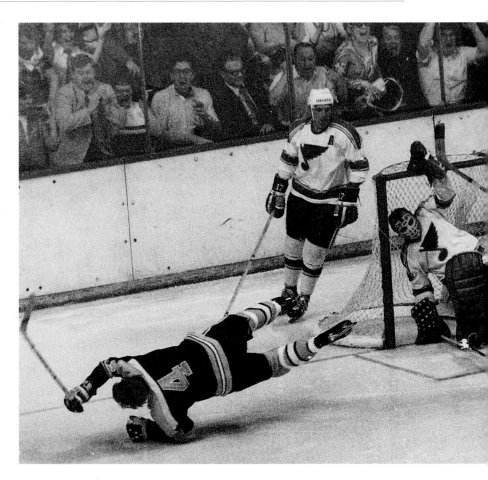

Orr's gravity-defying goal helped sweep the Bruins to the 1970 championships.

CANADA GETS A WAKEUP CALL

1972 Summit Series

In 1972, Canada's best hockey players were cocky. In 1972, Canada's hockey fans were even cockier. The NHL's players were nearly all Canadians and the pros were readily conceded to be the greatest players in the world.

When the NHL Players Association's executive director, Alan Eagleson, negotiated a complicated set of agreements that would allow the Canadians to face the Soviet Union national team, the consensus was that the NHL Canadian stars would rout the pride of a Communist empire. Sure, the Soviets had dominated the world championships and the Olympics. But in those events they were beating amateurs. The Soviets contended they were amateurs, too. But under the auspices of belonging to the army, the Soviets ate, drank, slept, and played next to each other—skating comrades arm in arm. They enjoyed privileges that few of their countrymen shared.

Four of the 8 games in the tournament were to be played in Montreal, Toronto, Winnipeg, and Vancouver, followed by 4 games in Moscow. Unfortunately, Bobby Orr was sidelined with knee surgery and Bobby Hull had jumped to the World Hockey Association. Many believed the Canadians would win all 8 games anyway. Many believed wrong.

What emerged was a brilliant, nerve-wracking, humbling, and exhilarating tournament for the Canadians. Canada lost the opener, 7–3, after taking a 2–0 lead at the Montreal Forum. The Canadians buttoned down their egos and worked for a 4–1 victory in Game Two. The Canadians were sure they had matters back under control. They were wrong. They led 4–2 in Winnipeg in Game Three, but the Russians bounced back for a tie. The Soviets followed with victories in Vancouver and in the first game in Moscow.

In all, it took twenty-eight days for the Canadian team to ultimately pull out a 4–3–1 series triumph. When it was over, the country was showering its love and adulation on a rather unlikely hero named Paul Henderson of the Toronto Maple Leafs. Henderson was a very good but not great player. And he was subjected to some unfair demands after the victory. But for a special week in September 1972, Henderson was the most heroic athlete in the world.

Henderson scored the game-winning goals in the sixth and seventh matches, with the goal in Game Seven arriving with fewer than three minutes remaining. In the final game, Canada had fallen behind, 5–3, late in the second period. Phil Esposito, the Canadian team's best player, sliced the lead to 5–4. And Yvon Cournoyer followed at 12:56 to tie the game. The Russian goal judge, however, did not flash the red goal light. The referee did signal a goal, but many fans, including Eagleson, didn't see it. He went ballistic, bumping into policemen. The police pushed back. Suddenly, an international incident was brewing. The police tried to drag the irate Eagleson away, but a number of players and others in Canada's contingent rescued him. Eagleson was brought across the ice to safety. Undaunted, he shook his fist at the goal judge in defiance.

With thirty-four seconds remaining in Game Eight...well, let's allow the great Foster Hewitt's call to be repeated: "Savard cleared the pass to Stapleton. He cleared to the open wing to Cournoyer. Cournoyer took a shot. The defenseman fell over, Liapkin. Cournoyer has it on the wing. There's a shot! Henderson makes a wild stab for it and fell. Here's another shot. Right in front. They score! Henderson has scored for Canada!"

Despite the Canadians' dramatic rebound, international hockey would never be the same. The Soviets had shown they were on a par with Canada's best. It was shocking. It was humbling. But the sport itself would benefit tremendously from the merger of hockey styles.

Until 1972, Canada believed it ruled hockey by divine right. Although Paul Henderson's goal lifted Canada to a thrilling last-game victory, the Soviets had showed the Canadians otherwise.

BROAD STREET BULLIES RULE

May 18, 1974

They were the scourge of hockey. Yet they were adored in the City of Brotherly Love. Many maintained they were nothing more than thugs who employed gangland tactics. Others contended that nobody sweated and worked any harder or gave any more of themselves to reach hockey's mountaintop.

The Philadelphia Flyers, also known as the Broad Street Bullies, were Stanley Cup champions in 1974 and 1975, the first modern-day expansion team to ascend to that throne. They were forever in trouble with league disciplinarians and criticized by pacifists. Nevertheless, through their commitment and energy, they pushed the boundaries of hockey fervor beyond the borders of the original six teams.

The exact point where good, tough hockey ends and goon tactics begin has never been precise. Granted, the Flyers slashed, punched, and sneered their way to a new level, but they were condemned for some of the same things the Boston Bruins were toasted for three years earlier. Throughout their struggle, the Flyers never apologized. Never.

The Flyers had a menagerie of fighters named Moose (Dupont), the Hammer (Dave Schultz), Big Bird (Don Saleski), and the Hound (Bob Kelly). They were rabid intimidators. One result was a spate of cases of a mysterious illness known as the Philly Flu, in which visiting players suddenly turned up lame or sick rather than play at the Spectrum. But it was their angelic-faced captain with the devil's pitchfork, Bobby Clarke, and their

stonewall goalie, Bernie Parent, who powered the team. They were coached by enigmatic Freddie "the Fog" Shero, who was both brilliant and bizarre.

The Flyers would enjoy many sweet moments. But no moment is quite as special as the first Stanley Cup, and that came May 18, 1974. The Flyers had advanced to the finals with a 7-game semifinal victory over the Rangers. They had outraged a national television audience that watched as Schultz had unmercifully beaten Dale Rolfe. The Rangers did not retaliate.

The Bruins were different. They could not be intimidated. But the Flyers did grab a 3-to-1 series lead before losing in Boston in Game Five. Clarke's overtime goal in Game Two in Boston was key. It returned home-ice advantage to the Flyers, who were virtually unbeatable at the Spectrum. And Game Six sent Philadelphia fans, in sore need of sports success, to hockey heaven.

The Flyers had often used a recording of Kate Smith's "God Bless America" before games and made much fanfare of what a superb record (36–3–1 at that point) they had with it. This time Smith showed up in person. She threw a punch in the air after she finished singing. The Spectrum went into a frenzy. She had delivered an emotional knockout.

The only goal the Flyers needed arrived in the opening period when Rick MacLeish deflected Dupont's shot from the point. Parent and his brilliant glove hand held on for a 1–0 victory. Almost two million people lined Center City for the parade to toast their champions.

The Flyers won a second Stanley Cup over Buffalo in 1975. They were the only team to beat the touring Central Red Army team the next season. In the first period of that game, Ed Van Impe chopped down the great Valery Kharlamov, and the Soviets refused to play until tour organizer Alan Eagleson threatened to withhold their money. Later, in 1979–80, they would set an NHL record with a 35-game unbeaten streak. They were the hometown heroes, but outside Philadelphia, the Flyers were vilified.

Hockey fans around North America hated the Flyers. But in Philadelphia, the Broad Street Bullies were beloved. Bobby Clarke became an icon and the team symbolized all that was right and wrong with the sport.

THE MIRACLE AT LAKE PLACID

1980 Winter Olympics
"Do you believe in miracles? Yes!"

Those are the immortal words Al Michaels shouted on ABC as the final seconds ticked away on perhaps the greatest upset in hockey history. It was the miracle of Lake Placid. The 1980 United States Olympic team, seeded seventh in the twelve-nation tournament, upset the Soviet Union 4–3 in the semifinals.

This was no ordinary Soviet Union team. This was the Big Red Machine. The best team in the world. The previous year, the Soviets had whipped the NHL All-Stars in the Challenge Cup. A month before the Olympics, they humiliated coach Herb Brooks' Americans, 10–3. They had the great Vladislav Tretiak in goal. Names such as Balderis, Makarov, Krutov, Fetisov, and the venerable Boris Mikhailov dominated a frightening lineup. The Americans were thought to have an outside shot at a bronze medal, nothing more.

These low expectations served Team USA well. The players were taken lightly. Few people around the world knew who they were. There was little pressure. But the Americans also had home-ice advantage, a

masterful strategy set forth by Brooks, and a work ethic and never-say-die attitude that would capture the hearts of a country.

Only four thousand people attended the Americans' first game at the Olympic Ice Center, a 2–2 tie with Sweden, held a day before Opening Ceremonies. It would be the only game the Americans didn't win, but it was also among the most dramatic. Bill Baker scored on a forty-five-foot (13.7m) slapper past Pelle Lindbergh with twenty-seven seconds left to tie.

The Czechs were up next and many observers had them penciled in for the silver medal behind the Soviets. Brooks will be remembered for his strategy of combining the Canadian system of dogged defense with the European free-flowing offense called a weave. He also gave some memorable locker-room speeches. Addressing Team USA before the Czech game, Brooks likened the opposing team to a tiger: "Go up to the tiger, spit in his eye, and shoot the bastard." They did, 7–3. They beat Norway, Romania, and West Germany to complete the opening round 4–0–1.

But the Russians, in the other group, went 5–0, ripping Japan 16–0 and the Netherlands 17–4 along the way. And don't forget the 10–3 blasting that the Russians gave the U.S. team four weeks earlier.

The two forces collided in the semifinals. It didn't take long for Krutov to deflect Kasatonov's point shot for a 1–0 lead. But Buzz Schneider surprised Tretiak moments later with a soft goal. Makarov put the Soviets back ahead, 2–1, but in the closing seconds of the opening period, Tretiak left a weak rebound and Mark Johnson scored.

When the Americans took the ice for the second period, they couldn't believe their eyes. Coach Viktor Tikhonov had replaced the great Tretiak with Vladimir Myshkin. The Soviets took a 3–2 lead and held a 30–10 shot advantage after two periods. But the third period belonged to Jim Craig and the superbly conditioned Americans. Johnson tied the game at 8:39 with his second goal. And captain Mike Eruzione, who almost wasn't even invited to the tryouts, followed with a moment for the ages. Mark Pavelich found Eruzione with a pass at the top of the circle, and using the Russian defense as a screen, Eruzione scored the go-ahead goal. Craig stopped everything else.

Brooks skated the Americans like dogs the following morning to make sure they didn't get cocky before the gold-medal game against Finland. He told his players if they lost this one they'd take it to their graves. The Americans didn't let up. They won the game, 4–2, and the gold medal. Michaels spoke for all when he shouted: "The impossible dream comes true!"

Do you believe in miracles? That was the only question after Herb Brooks, Jim Craig, and Mike Eruzione became household names with the Americans' 1980 gold-medal victory at Lake Placid.

THE GREATEST HOCKEY EVER

1987 Canada Cup

On the eve of the final game, Jean Perron, one of Team Canada's coaches, warned bystanders to brace themselves for total awe. "Buckle your seat belts," Perron said, "for a trip into hockey space."

The 1987 Canada Cup tournament was the greatest hockey ever played. Although Alan Eagleson has been severely criticized for his role as the players' union chief and faces federal indictments for alleged fraud, he can be proud of the Canada Cup, which was his baby. He nurtured it through its formative years in the 1970s and he survived the cruel 8–1 loss Canada suffered at the hands of the Soviet Union in the 1981 final.

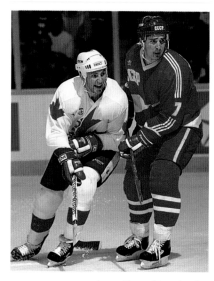

The 1987 tournament turned out to be the last appearance for the Big Red Machine against the NHL's best. After the fall of Communism, it just wasn't the same.

Was there a winner? The scoreboard will recall three 6–5 games, two decided in overtime and the last one decided with eighty-four seconds remaining. Mario Lemieux, moved from center to Wayne Gretzky's right wing by coach Mike Keenan, scored the winning goal for Canada. The sides met four times, including a 3–3 tie in the round robin, and one measly goal separated them. Would it have been different if Moscow was the venue? Maybe. Maybe not.

All of Canada celebrated. Copps Coliseum in Hamilton, Ontario, was filled with red and white that night. Thousands of flags waved in the building. Young fans painted their faces half red and half white, and finished off their makeup with a maple leaf.

Each game was crisp and brilliantly played. The Canadians did establish their superior corner work, but did not stoop to thuggery. The Soviets, robotic and stiff in the past, were much more human. They cel-ebrated goals. They argued with the referees. They showed an ability to bounce back. The passing? The shooting? The stickwork? The skating? All done brilliantly. The players were stars shining in the hockey galaxy.

Gretzky, Lemieux, Coffey, Bourque, Messier, Fuhr...they were all there for Team Canada. So were Dale Hawerchuck and Normand Rochefort, who played underrated roles in the victory. The Soviets were also stacked. But Gretzky and Lemieux came out on top. Gretzky set tournament records for assists and points. Lemieux had 4 game-winning goals as Number 66 accounted for 66 percent of the Canadians' victory. Lemieux set a tournament record for 11 goals. Gretzky set up 9 of them.

Game One at Montreal Forum was a dandy. Alexander Semak scored at 5:33 of overtime to lift the Soviets to a win. Game Two at Copps Coliseum was arguably the greatest game ever played. The Canadians took a 3–1 lead in the first period. But they blew the lead twice, and with sixty-four seconds left, Valery Kamensky danced through the entire Canadian team to score an incredible tying goal. Then at 10:07 of the second overtime, Lemieux had his first of two decisive responses to the Russians' effrontery.

The Canadians fell behind 3–0 early in Game Three and there was talk of a rout to rival the 1981 disaster. Not this time. Number 99 and Number 66 would have the last say. With 1:24 remaining, off a face-off draw near Canada's blue line, Gretzky rushed down the left wing into the Soviets. He held patiently until Lemieux found a hole. Hawerchuk got away with hooking Viacheslav Bykov to spring Lemieux. Gretzky fed a perfect pass to Lemieux, who lifted a wicked wrist shot over goalie Sergei Mylnikov's glove for the glory of Canada.

With the fall of Communism, almost all the top Russians are playing in the NHL as teammates of Canadians and Americans. The 1987 Canada Cup furnished the last and, some say, the best showdown between East and West.

GRETZKY SURPASSES HOWE

October 15, 1989

It may be argued that Wayne Gretzky's entire career was one prolonged greatest moment. Night after night, month after month, season after season, the Great One kept producing magical moments. Gretzky set records, broke his own marks, and then did it again.

He won four Stanley Cups with the Edmonton Oilers. He broke Phil Esposito's goal and points record for a single season. He smashed Bobby Orr's single-season assist record. He went on to break every one of Gordie Howe's career scoring marks. The list is endless.

But no moment could match October 15, 1989, for its sheer drama. Oh, there was little doubt that Number 99 would overtake Howe's career mark of 1,850 points. But the manner in which Gretzky accomplished the feat was nothing short of beautiful.

Although he had been traded to the Los Angeles Kings in August 1988, Gretzky managed to save the surpassing moment for his return to Edmonton when the Kings were going up against the Oilers at Northlands Coliseum. This was the place that the Great One had filled and thrilled for a decade. Gretzky would not disappoint the 17,503 fans who jammed the arena to cheer their favorite son. It didn't matter that he had been in Hollywood for fourteen months. For this one night, he belonged to Edmonton again.

Gretzky entered the game with 1,849 points. It took him only four minutes and thirty-two seconds to tie Howe as he picked up an assist on Bernie Nicholls' goal. But with less than four minutes to go, Nicholls rang a shot off the post, dashing Gretzky's hopes for another assist. It looked as if Gretzky was done for the night.

Gordie Howe and Wayne Gretzky have always maintained a special friendship, which remains despite Gretzky's breaking all of Howe's important career scoring records.

But that would have been anticlimactic, and Gretzky is nothing if not the master of the dramatic. He took matters into his own hands. With a minute to go, the Kings pulled goalie Mario Gosselin for an extra attacker. There was a face-off in the Edmonton end. Mark Messier won the face-off draw, but Kevin Lowe was unable to clear the puck out of the Oiler defensive zone. Los Angeles defenseman Steve Duchesne kept the puck alive inside the blue line and sent it back toward the goal. The puck bounced over Lowe's stick and hit Dave Taylor's knee, and suddenly, Gretzky was alone in front with the puck.

In a flash, the puck was behind Oiler goalie Bill Ranford. Only fifty-three seconds remained in regulation play. Wrapped up in the moment, the fans erupted as if one of their own had scored the goal. Indeed, he was one of theirs, even though Number 99 was wearing an opposing uniform. The number 1,851 flashed on and off on the score-

board. The game was stopped. The red carpet was rolled out. Gretzky's dad, Walter, gave him a big hug. Howe, who had followed Gretzky around, offered his congratulations. The Oilers, represented by Gretzky's good friend Messier, and the Kings gave him gifts. Messier and Gretzky hugged. NHL President John Ziegler paid his tribute. Kings owner Bruce McNall and Gretzky's wife, actress Janet Jones, stepped on the ice, too. Graciously, Howe called Gretzky "a superb hockey player and a superb young man. He calls me a friend and that's one of the greatest things in my life."

Another guy would have called it a night and basked in the glory. Not Gretzky. He kissed his wife and went back to work. Incredibly, with 1:36 remaining in overtime, Gretzky scored another goal for point number 1,852—and won the game, too. "This will be the highlight of my life," Gretzky said.

ENDING THE RANGERS CURSE

June 21, 1994

It was a drought. It was a curse. And every time Islanders fans chanted "1940! 1940!" it caused pain for Rangers fans.

Was there really a curse on the Rangers? Some insisted the hockey gods were punishing the Rangers for burning Madison Square Garden's $3 million mortgage in the bowl of the Stanley Cup. You can kiss the Stanley Cup. You can hoist the Stanley Cup over your head. You can drink champagne from it and sleep with it. But never be so crass as General John Reed Kilpatrick was in using the Stanley Cup as a furnace in early 1941.

Seasons passed. Players and coaches, twenty-four coaches to be exact, came and went. There were births and deaths, bar mitzvahs and marriages. Rangers fans remained forever loyal and forever frustrated.

Andy Bathgate and Harry Howell, Vic Hadfield and Jean Ratelle, Rod Gilbert and Brad Park, Emile Francis and Fred Shero. John Davidson as a goalie and Davidson as a broadcaster. The historical roster went on and on. The Islanders owned the Stanley Cup in the early 1980s. Four in a row, in fact. Only grandpa remembered 1940, the last time the Rangers held Lord Stanley's treasure.

That curse (or whatever it was) was finally, mercifully, lifted on June 21, 1994, after an incredible 4,150-game drought. It couldn't have come at a better time for hockey. The NBA was dawdling through a listless playoff season. Baseball faced a long and costly strike. The NHL was suddenly a hot item.

There were three major reasons why things looked good for the Rangers this time:

No defenseman since Bobby Orr combined offensive flair with defensive responsibility like Brian Leetch.

Coach Mike Keenan, who would leave the Rangers just days later after an ugly spat with general manager Neil Smith, proved to be the perfect taskmaster for a one-year winning stretch. Keenan had been to the finals three times previously without taking home the Cup.

Mark Messier led a group of seven former Edmonton Oilers, who combined had twenty-six Stanley Cup rings. And Messier, dubbed the Messiah by the New York tabloids, put on a fabulous show.

The Rangers blitzed the Islanders and the Washington Capitals in the first two rounds. Three times they faced elimination in the final two series, including Games Six and Seven in the semifinals against the New Jersey Devils.

Messier guaranteed a victory before Game Six, leading to an immediate comparison to Joe Namath's prediction of a Jets victory before Super Bowl III. But when the Devils assumed a 2–0 lead, Messier's forecast appeared inaccurate. But Messier set up Alexei Kovalev for a goal and followed with 3 goals of his own in the third period for the victory. It was the first playoff hat trick of Messier's career. It also was the stuff of legend. The Devils' Valeri Zelepukin scored with 7.7 seconds remaining to send Game Seven into overtime. But Stephane Matteau would score his second overtime goal of the series to push the Rangers to the finals.

Racing to a 3–1 final series lead against Vancouver, the Rangers appeared to be coasting. But to the consternation of Rangers fans, the long-awaited moment was delayed when the Canucks won Game Five at the Garden and returned home to win Game Six. The Canucks used a hyperbaric oxygen chamber as their secret weapon. The chamber is said to reduce fatigue and fight injuries. But in the end, no hyperbaric chamber could stop destiny. The tense 3–2 victory in Game Seven may have been the sixth Stanley Cup ring for Messier, Kevin Lowe, and Glenn Anderson. But it was the first for the Rangers in fifty-four years.

Many Rangers fans believed their team was cursed forever. But by the time they saw goalie Mike Richter lift the Stanley Cup, they knew fifty-four years of pain and agony were finally over.

The 1929 Boston Bruins won the Stanley Cup by allowing only 9 goals in 5 successive playoff wins.

THE DYNASTIES

Maybe it is something in the grassroots character of the Canadian boys who have dominated hockey for the better part of a century. Their egos are tiny compared with those of players in other major league sports. They are fraternal. The inner workings of their locker room is the very essence of team spirit.

Maybe it is that unlike in other sports leagues, which tend to focus more on individual players (the NBA, especially, is a collection of individual stars), the team is everything in the NHL.

Maybe it is the nature of the sport itself. Hockey calls for crisp passing, organized defensive coverage, concise breakout patterns, and emotional play.

Or maybe the talent pool and number of teams were just so small over the years compared with those of baseball, football, and basketball that it was inevitable certain teams would come to dominate the sport.

Whatever the reason, certain teams have played a crucial role in the history of the National Hockey League.

Call the best ones the Dynasties.

How do you define a dynasty? Many hockey pundits say a team must win three Stanley Cup titles in a row to lay claim to the title.

In that case, the Edmonton Oilers of the 1980s would not qualify—and that is clearly wrong. The Oilers did not play in an era when there were only six teams. The odds of a team winning it all were significantly better in those days.

And the Oilers did win the Stanley Cup five times in seven seasons. Wayne Gretzky, Mark Messier, Paul Coffey, Jari Kurri, Glenn Anderson, Kevin Lowe, and Grant Fuhr will be remembered for helping to form the greatest offensive team in hockey history. Led by the ultra confident Glen Sather, the Oilers were a swashbuckling, fun-loving bunch who set the oil fields of Alberta ablaze.

The New York Islanders, who immediately preceded the Oilers as a dynasty, could beat their opponents regardless of their style of play. They were tough. They were offensively gifted. They were defensively stingy. And Billy Smith furnished terrific clutch goaltending.

But it is the 1956–60 Montreal Canadiens that folks reserve for the title of the greatest dynasty. They had no weaknesses.

The Detroit Red Wings of the early 1950s were the best team left off our list of five dynasties. They won seven regular season titles in a row in a six-team league. And with Gordie Howe, Ted Lindsay, Terry Sawchuk, and Red Kelly, folks in Motown will undoubtedly say we're crazy for leaving them out.

And what about the Central Red Army, (the Soviet national team,) and the 1980 U.S. Olympic team? They could be considered possible dynasties, too. It's just impossible to judge them since they were essentially All-Star teams and did not stand the grueling test of a complete NHL season and playoff.

THE 1956-60 MONTREAL CANADIENS

They were the greatest team in hockey history. And if you care to argue otherwise, you will be at a great disadvantage.

How great were they? In 1960, the Montreal Canadiens became the only team ever to capture the Stanley Cup five years in a row. And they finished with the best record in the NHL's regular season for four of those five seasons.

It is a measuring stick of greatness when other teams gang up on the champions to create rules specifically designed to call a halt to their winning ways. The NHL pulled this stunt before the 1956–57 season when member teams voted to change rules regarding the power play.

Until this time, a player receiving a minor penalty would serve the entire two minutes. The Canadiens would often strike twice, even three times, with a fearsome power-play unit. The Canadiens, in fact, scored a quarter of their goals with the man advantage. In 1956, the NHL voted to allow the penalized player to rejoin play after one power-play goal. The Canadiens nevertheless went on to capture the Stanley Cup four more times.

The Canadiens simply did not have a weakness. And under the legendary Toe Blake, the coach who came on board in 1956, the Canadiens were able to blend zealous youngsters with seasoned veterans and control the violent tempers of Rocket Richard and Boom Boom Geoffrion in the process.

Jacques Plante was a brilliant goalie. Critics called him a hypochondriac, and his behavior was sometimes bizarre—but he won the Vezina Trophy for the NHL's best goals-against average all five times during the Canadiens' Stanley Cup reign.

On defense, there were Doug Harvey and Tom Johnson. Four times during this run, Harvey was named the recipient of the Norris Trophy as the league's premier defenseman. Johnson, severely underrated, won it the other time. Although the younger generation would certainly say Bobby Orr is the greatest defenseman of all time and the old-timers would counter with Eddie Shore's name, Harvey ranks high among the best in history.

But French Canadiens fans reserve their most passionate love for their own. And up front, there was a foursome that helped coin the term "Firewagon Hockey." Their press, press, press, press offense made them thrilling. And as a result, they are often compared in offensive brilliance to baseball's 1927 New York Yankees.

There was Maurice Richard, fiery and temperamental on the ice, and a loner, almost a brooder, off the ice. There was his little brother, Henri, the "Pocket Rocket," a rookie in 1955–56, who would go on to win a record eleven Stanley Cups. Maurice was in his mid-thirties. Henri was only nineteen. Together with Dickie Moore, who led the league in scoring twice, they formed a dynamic line.

This left Jean Beliveau and Boom Boom Geoffrion on an equally prolific line with Bert Olmstead. With the Richards and Beliveau dazzling, Olmstead doing the grunt work up front, and Harvey and Geoffrion on the points, it is clear to see why the power play was so devastating. Beliveau was incredibly smooth, a gentleman always, and one of the greatest centermen and passers ever. Geoffrion, who revolutionized the slap shot, got his nickname from the sounds he made. The first boom was his stick hitting the puck. The second boom was the puck exploding against the rear boards.

They were the perfect team. And the 1956–60 Canadiens grew accustomed to hoisting coach Toe Blake and the Stanley Cup above their heads.

THE 1984-90 EDMONTON OILERS

No other team in NHL history has scored 400 goals in one season. The Edmonton Oilers did it five times, peaking at 446 in 1984. These boys could score goals at a pace more alarming than anybody since they first started games of pond shinny.

At the heart of all this was a skinny kid from Brantford, Ontario. Wayne Gretzky, who moved into the NHL in 1979 from the dismantled World Hockey Association, proved as elusive as he was dynamic. Defenders found they couldn't stop what they couldn't hit, and Gretzky simply kept pouring in goals and setting up his winger, Jari Kurri.

Gretzky was always friendly, accessible, and respectful. But the Oilers were a young, cocky bunch. They had fun. They liked to run and gun and leave goalie Grant Fuhr on his own to bail them out.

At first, the Oilers were often a joke defensively. Paul Coffey could score like no defenseman in the history of hockey, but he'd abandon his position too frequently to roam the ice. But as the seasons went on, the Oilers matured. So did their game. They buckled down defensively when needed.

The Oilers never won three Stanley Cups in a row. Some pundits claim "three-peating" is the true mark of a dynasty. But the Oilers' accomplishment of five in seven years ranks with the best. The fourth Cup came in 1988, without Coffey, who was traded away after one too many spats with general manager and coach Glen Sather. The fifth Cup came without Gretzky, dealt to Los Angeles in a trade that shocked the

sports world. This fifth win obviously speaks volumes about those who remained.

Mark Messier started out as a big, raw-boned kid. He developed into one of the strongest, most charismatic leaders in the sport. His teammates claimed you could see victory in his eyes. He became transfixed. His incredible will, his powerful body and skating stride, and his powerful wrist shot could always be counted on in the most crucial moments.

Fuhr's numbers will never compare with those of the original six teams' goalies. The Oilers abandoned defense on many nights and Fuhr's attention span would wander at times. But as far as quickness of reflex and clutch play, few goalies were ever better. Kevin Lowe was a dependable, mature force on defense. Enigmatic Glenn Anderson was another matter on wing. Too often his concentration would waver during the season. But Anderson also used amazing foot speed to score some of Edmonton's most crucial playoff goals.

Sather used brawlers like Dave Semenko, Kevin McClelland, and Marty McSorley to protect Gretzky. He used Esa Tikkanen to agitate and check, along with Craig MacTavish, who was successfully rehabilitated after a drunken-driving conviction involving a fatality. Sather could incorporate such European talents as Reijo Ruotsalainen, Kent Nilsson, and Petr Klima—and discard them just as easily. Sather used the remnants of the Gretzky and Jimmy Carson (who arrived in the Gretzky deal) trades to acquire such kids as Adam Graves, Joe Murphy,

and Martin Gelinas, and to squeeze out one more Stanley Cup in 1990. Craig Simpson, who arrived in the Coffey deal from Pittsburgh, scored a whopping 30 playoff goals in the final half of the glory era.

Why didn't they go on to win six or seven successive Cups? Owner Peter Pocklington's financial problems caused the Oilers to eventually sell off their best talent. It became impossible to pay everybody. In 1986, teammate Steve Smith banked a shot off the unsuspecting Fuhr in a Game Seven playoff loss to Calgary. It was a stunning moment that led to elimination. But this explains only one loss. In the end, lack of money ended the Oilers' reign.

Coach Glen Sather was cocky and so was his group of swashbuckling Edmonton Oilers in the 1980s. Led by Wayne Gretzky's wizardry, the Oilers were the greatest offensive machine in NHL history.

THE 1980-83 NEW YORK ISLANDERS

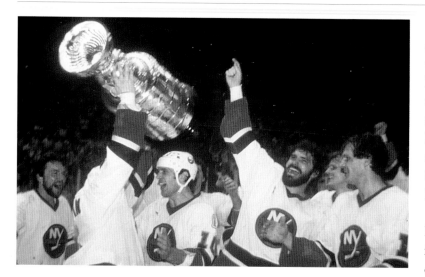

They were transformed from Team Choke into an invincible force that could defeat an opponent by any weapon of its choice.

Was the winning strategy to try to outscore the New York Islanders? Mike Bossy, Bryan Trottier, and Denis Potvin had the answer. Was it to pull a Philadelphia Flyer brawl and try to bully the Islanders? Clark Gillies, Bobby Nystrom, and Gary Howatt could answer any bell for belligerence. And the Islanders' potent power play would answer stupid penalties.

The Islanders had offense, defense, and special teams. Backing up all this talent was Battlin' Billy Smith, an arrogant, mean-spirited goalie who would stop anything fired his way in the playoffs. He also was known to chop his stick at an opponent's ankle or chin.

When a crucial goal was needed, Nystrom delivered the goods, including the Stanley Cup clincher in overtime of Game Six in the 1980 finals against the Flyers. In all, Nystrom scored 4 overtime playoff goals in his career. Center Butch Goring, who was named the Conn Smythe Trophy winner in 1981 for outstanding playoff performer, held the opponents' best scorers in check and scored many crucial points. And Bob Bourne, as fast a skater as there was in the NHL, pitched in his share of big plays, too.

The Islanders won nineteen successive playoff series, including some memorable wars with the rival New York Rangers, before they tumbled in the 1984 championship series to the young, swashbuckling Edmonton Oilers. And in doing so, the Islanders carved out an important niche in NHL history. Although the Flyers had become the first modern-day expansion club to capture the Stanley Cup a few years earlier, the Islanders became the prototype for building a franchise from scratch and nurturing it into a dynasty. General manager Bill Torrey, known for his big bow ties, deftly used top picks to construct a superbly balanced club.

Potvin grew into the best defenseman of the late 1970s. Bossy may have been the greatest shooter ever. And Trottier, Bossy's center, was a force both in his end and in front of his opponent's net. Over the years, others fit in nicely. Stefan Persson, Mike McEwen, and Tomas Jonsson added offense to the backline. Ken Morrow, one of the golden boys from the 1980 U.S. Olympic miracle team, was a steady rudder. Dave Langevin and Gord Lane furnished the muscle. Up front, every night was a passion play for John Tonelli and the Sutter boys, Duane and Brent. Gillies was a sleeping giant, a serious physical and offensive force when aroused.

Torrey annually made deadline moves that seemed to propel the Islanders. The most memorable came in 1980 when he sent Billy Harris and Dave Lewis to the Los Angeles Kings for Goring. Goring had a scraggly beard and hair and wore a little, battered helmet. But he was a beautiful complement as number two center behind Trottier.

The Islanders' poise and grace under pressure is a sign of their maturity and a tribute to their even-tempered coach, Al Arbour. But there was a time when it looked as if the Islanders would never shake off the early shackles of Team Choke. They surpassed 100 points in the regular season standings four successive seasons and advanced to the playoff semifinals four times in five years. But each time, the Islanders fell short. Finally, they stunned the Flyers in the 1980 final after the Flyers had set an NHL record with a 35-game unbeaten streak during the regular season. The dynasty had begun.

Mike Bossy scored goals and lifted Stanley Cups above his head. Denis Potvin could control a game all over the ice. The Islanders, in short, could beat you any way you wanted to play.

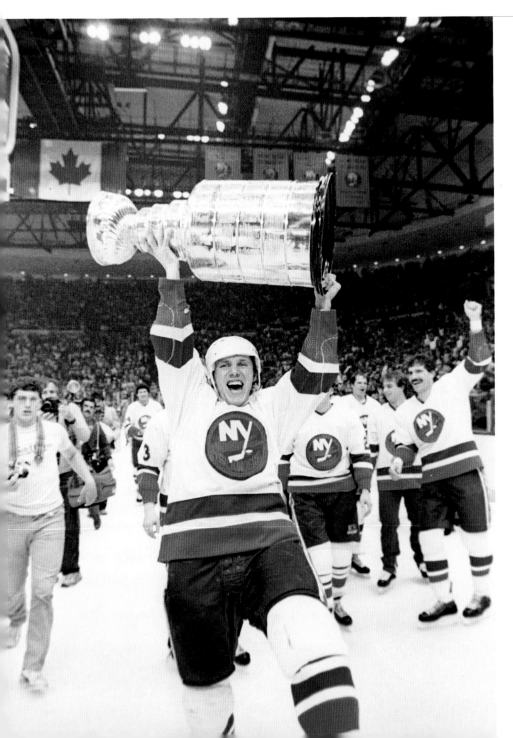

THE 1976-79 MONTREAL CANADIENS

Some say it was Flower power. Some say it was the Big Three on D. Others say it was the gangly, studious gentleman in goal. Still others maintain it was the taskmaster behind the bench.

In truth, it was all of these that enabled the Montreal Canadiens to capture four successive Stanley Cup championships from 1976 through 1979. Impressive though that record is, they did more: the Habs built the best regular-season records in modern hockey history.

Consider these monuments to domination: In 1975–76, the Canadiens set NHL records with 58 wins, 127 points, and 26 road victories. In 1976–77, the Canadiens promptly went out and broke all the records of the previous season with 60 wins, 132 points, and 27 road victories. The Canadiens had gone 60–8–12. Whoever said "you can't win 'em all" wasn't right by much.

There is one mitigating factor, however. The World Hockey Association had raided many of the NHL's best players during this period. Add to that a number of expansion teams, and the overall balance of the league was diluted. On too many nights, the Canadiens simply had to throw their sticks on the ice, and some weak opponent would throw up the white flag of surrender.

This doesn't mean there weren't formidable opponents, including Philadelphia, Boston, Buffalo, and New York. The Flyers, in fact, presented the Canadiens with one of the most riveting finals in NHL history. It was 1976. In the minds of many fans, the two-time defending champion Flyers were the essence of evil, goons who had brawled and snarled their way to success.

To those fans, the Canadiens were the good guys. With Guy "The Flower" Lafleur leading the attack, Montreal seemed to represent the essence of artistry in the sport. Indeed, Lafleur would emerge as the game's premier player over the next few years. But in the 1976 finals, it was towering defenseman Larry Robinson who was a hero for stand-

ing up to the Flyers' Dave "The Hammer" Schultz. The Canadiens would not be intimidated.

Although they didn't have a Bobby Orr, no team ever had a better trio of defenseman than Robinson, Serge Savard, and Guy Lapointe. "One of the them was on the ice all the time," said Emile Francis, who ran the Rangers and the Blues during the 1970s. "They always seemed to be in control of the game."

In goal, Ken Dryden looked like a giraffe. He studied law; he became an author; he even quit for one season to go to school. But during this period, Dryden did nothing but win.

Jacques Lemaire was an underrated, splendid center for Lafleur. Steve Shutt, on left wing, scored a bundle of goals. Interestingly, the player who was most admired by the the Soviets during this period was a fellow named Bob Gainey. The Soviets, who had emerged as a world hockey power, called Gainey technically the best player in the world. He didn't score all that much. But he may have been the best defensive forward in NHL history.

Once they toppled the Flyers and were toasted by the hockey world for whipping The Bullies, the Canadiens were seriously threatened only a couple of times. The most riveting moment came in 1979 in Game Seven of the semifinals. The Bruins—Don Cherry's Lunchpail A.C. boys—had the Canadiens down a goal in the closing minutes. But a too-many-men-on-the-ice penalty led to a Lafleur power-play goal. Lafleur's shot seemed to break the sound barrier. And Yvon Lambert's overtime goal finished off the Bruins.

In 1975, Henri Richard had retired at age thirty-nine—the same age at which his brother, Maurice, had retired—severing the final tie to the Canadiens' storied past. Richard had won eleven Stanley Cups, dating to 1956. It was time for the young bucks to emerge. And they did. It was the beginning of a new era. In turn, it was Dryden's retirement and coach Scotty Bowman's depature after the Canadiens' fourth Stanley Cup that signaled the end of another great reign.

Ken Dryden, Guy Lafleur, and the rest of the superbly coached 1976–79 Canadiens celebrated four Stanley Cups in a row.

THE 1962-67 TORONTO MAPLE LEAFS

Maybe they aren't one of the five best teams of all time. Maybe the Detroit Red Wings, who won seven regular-season titles and four Stanley Cups between 1949 and 1955, were better. Maybe the Maple Leafs of the immediate post–World War II era were better. After all, they won three Stanley Cups in a row, too.

But, then again, the Maple Leafs of the early 1960s could beat anybody in hockey on a given night. This was a fascinating collection of men. They didn't have a dominating superstar, not in the category of Wayne Gretzky, Bobby Orr, or Gordie Howe. And they won only one regular-season title during their best run.

So what makes them so great? They rose to the occasion. They seized the spring moment for three Stanley Cups in a row in 1962, 1963, and 1964, and they added a fourth one in 1967. Remember, these were the final days before the size of the NHL doubled from six to twelve teams in 1967.

Although they didn't have any superstars, their roster was filled with players who would eventually enter the Hockey Hall of Fame. The way they made it there was fascinating. Many would contend that with

the irascible Punch Imlach serving as general manager and coach, they got there by being pushed and prodded, yelled and screamed at.

Take goalie Johnny Bower. He had played for the New York Rangers in 1954, but had disappeared to the minors before reemerging under Imlach's coaching. Allan Stanley's play often had been lackluster in other NHL towns. He had earned the particular wrath of Madison Square Garden fans while he was with the Rangers. But in Toronto he became a leader, and paired with Tim Horton, he was an immense physical presence.

But Imlach's most compelling move was acquiring Red Kelly from Detroit and turning him from a defenseman into a center. Kelly, one of the game's best on defense, had fallen into the doghouse with Red Wing boss Jack Adams. Imlach's bold move to get Kelly worked. His plan was to use Kelly as a center to try to slow Jean Beliveau, the great center of the Montreal Canadiens. In the process, Kelly found a second career as an outstanding center.

One by one, Imlach revived careers and merged the oldsters with the stockpile of young talent. Dave Keon centered Dick Duff and cap-

Pulled out of the minors, aging goalie Johnny Bower (above) led the Leafs to four Stanley Cups.

tain George Armstrong. Today that would form one heck of a number one line for most teams. But another line, made up of Kelly, Frank Mahovlich, and Bob Nevin, gave Imlach terrific punch. Later, Andy Bathgate was put with Kelly and Mahovlich, and the line helped power the Leafs to their third Stanley Cup, in 1964. Bathgate, however, was traded a year after Imlach got him because he complained about Imlach's tactics. Bob Pulford, Bert Olmstead, and Eddie Shack gave the Leafs a tenacious third line.

Imlach's demanding ways and fierce demeanor took a toll on his troops. Eventually, insurrections among the players would cause the Leafs' demise. But not before a few legendary tales were told. Game Six of the 1964 Stanley Cup finals best exemplified this group's grit and ability to rise to greatness. Defenseman Bobby Baun broke his leg. He should have left the game. Instead, he took painkillers and went back on the ice. He scored the winning goal in overtime. That one kept ol' Punch happy.

HOCKEY CHRONOLOGY

1893: For $48.67, Lord Stanley buys and donates a silver punch bowl for hockey competition. Montreal AAA wins the initial challenge.

1910: The format of the game changes from two 30-minute halves to three 20-minute periods.

1919: The Montreal-Seattle Stanley Cup final is called off because of an influenza epidemic that claims the life of Montreal's Joe Hall.

1922: The immortal Foster Hewitt broadcasts the first NHL game on radio.

1927: The NHL institutes a rule that allows only the team captain to address the referee during a game.

1930: It becomes mandatory for each player to wear a number at least 10 inches (25cm) high on the back of the sweater.

1936: Montreal Maroons' Russ Blinco becomes the first NHL player ever to wear eyeglasses in a game.

1940: The Ross-Tyer puck is adopted as the NHL's official puck—but early in the season it is deemed too soft and is replaced by the Spalding puck.

1944: Rocket Richard is named first, second, and third star of the Stanley Cup final game when he scores all 5 Montreal goals in a victory over Toronto.

1947: Although a onetime event for the benefit of Ace Bailey was held in 1933, the first of what would become the annual NHL All-Star Game is held in Toronto.

1953: The Cleveland Barons, champions of the American League, challenge the NHL champions. The NHL refuses the challenge.

1911: The rules change when the National Hockey Association, predecessor of the National Hockey League, drops the rover position and replaces a seven-man game with a six-man game.

1917: The NHL is organized on November 22. The Montreal Canadiens, Montreal Wanderers, Ottawa Senators, Quebec Bulldogs, and Toronto Arenas join the new league, although Quebec does not start until 1919 and the Wanderers withdraw when their arena burns.

1923: Boston becomes the first American city to be awarded an NHL team.

1925: Hamilton finishes first in the NHL standings, getting into the finals. But the team's players, demanding $200 for each additional game, go on strike. The franchise folds.

1934: Because of the Depression, the maximum team payroll is dropped from $70,000 to $62,500 and the maximum player salary is dropped from $7,500 to $7,000.

1936: Maple Leafs–Canadiens game is postponed on January 21 after death of King George V. It is the first such tribute in NHL history.

1942: The Brooklyn Americans withdraw from the NHL, leaving a six-team league in place for the next 25 years.

1942: Because of wartime restrictions on train scheduling, regular season overtime is discontinued.

1949: Ice is painted white.

1952: Cleveland applies for an NHL franchise, but the application is denied.

1954: Each arena is required to operate an out-of-town scoreboard.

1955: Referees begin wearing shirts with vertical black-and-white stripes because their orange sweaters look all black on black and white television, making it difficult for watchers to distinguish between referees and players.

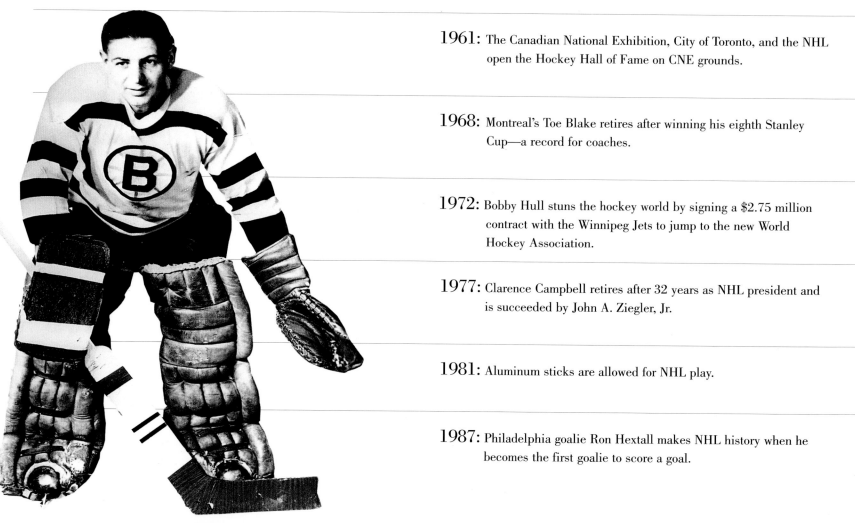

1956: The Montreal power play is so devastating that the NHL creates a new rule allowing a player to come out of the penalty box after 1 man-advantage goal.

1958: Players are permitted to wear plastic protective masks while recovering from facial injuries.

1961: The Canadian National Exhibition, City of Toronto, and the NHL open the Hockey Hall of Fame on CNE grounds.

1968: Montreal's Toe Blake retires after winning his eighth Stanley Cup—a record for coaches.

1972: Bobby Hull stuns the hockey world by signing a $2.75 million contract with the Winnipeg Jets to jump to the new World Hockey Association.

1977: Clarence Campbell retires after 32 years as NHL president and is succeeded by John A. Ziegler, Jr.

1981: Aluminum sticks are allowed for NHL play.

1987: Philadelphia goalie Ron Hextall makes NHL history when he becomes the first goalie to score a goal.

1960: Twenty years before Jim Craig and the U.S. Olympic team become household names, Jack McCartan leads the U.S. to the gold at Squaw Valley.

1964: The Conn Smythe Trophy is instituted for the most valuable player in the playoffs. Jean Beliveau is the first winner.

1967: The Original Six is doubled as the NHL undergoes its first major expansion.

1969: The amateur draft is expanded to include all amateur players of qualifying age throughout the world. The number one pick is Rejean Houle by Montreal.

1970: Home teams are allowed to put their names on the back of team jerseys; visitors need the home team's consent. Seven years later, names become mandatory.

1974: Kate Smith sings "God Bless America" at the Spectrum to inspire the Philadelphia Flyers to take the Stanley Cup.

1976: Toronto's Darryl Sittler sets the NHL record with 10 points in a game against Boston.

1979: The World Hockey Association dissolves. Quebec, Hartford, Edmonton, and Winnipeg are brought into the NHL.

1981: The Soviet Union whips Canada, 8–1, in the Canada Cup final, plunging the entire country into mourning.

1983: Five-minute, sudden-death overtime is instituted for regular season games.

1985: Philadelphia goalie Pelle Lindbergh, one of hockey's top young players, is killed when his Porsche crashes into a New Jersey wall.

1988: Mario Lemieux becomes the only player other than Wayne Gretzky to win the NHL's Most Valuable Player award since Bryan Trottier in 1979.

1988: An irate New Jersey coach Jim Schoenfeld yells at referee Don Koharski: "Have another doughnut, you fat pig!" When officials refuse to work the next Devils playoff game, they are replaced by local amateurs wearing yellow practice jerseys.

1989: Sergei Priakin becomes the first Soviet Union player permitted to sign with an NHL club.

1991: The NHL institutes video replays to assist referees for goal–no goal calls.

1992: Ten-day players strike in April threatens cancellation of playoffs before last-minute settlement.

1992: The NHL turns to the National Basketball Association for its new leader. Gary Bettman is named the first commissioner.

1993: Disney and Blockbuster Video get into the action as the NHL expands into Anaheim with the Mighty Ducks and into Miami with the Florida Panthers.

1994: An NHL lockout lasts 101 days, forcing cancellation of 36 of each team's regularly scheduled 84 games.

HOCKEY HALL OF FAME

There are 296 members in the Hockey Hall of Fame.
Here are the 203 who were inducted in the
players category.

Sid Abel	Rusty Crawford	Riley Hern	Lanny McDonald	Ernest Russell
Jack Adams	Jack Darragh	Bryan Hextall	Frank McGee	Jack Ruttan
Syl Apps	Scotty Davidson	Hap Holmes	Billy McGimsie	Serge Savard
George Armstrong	Hap Day	Tom Hooper	George McNamara	Terry Sawchuk
Ace Bailey	Alex Delvecchio	Red Horner	Stan Mikita	Fred Scanlan
Dan Bain	Cy Denneny	Tim Horton	Dickie Moore	Milt Schmidt
Hobey Baker	Marcel Dionne	Gordie Howe	Paddy Moran	Sweeney Schriner
Bill Barber	Gordon Drillon	Syd Howe	Howie Morenz	Earl Seibert
Marty Barry	Charlie Drinkwater	Harry Howell	Bill Mosienko	Oliver Seibert
Andy Bathgate	Ken Dryden	Bobby Hull	Frank Nighbor	Eddie Shore
Jean Beliveau	Woody Dumart	Bouse Hutton	Reg Noble	Steve Shutt
Clint Benedict	Tom Dunderdale	Harry Hyland	Buddy O'Connor	Babe Siebert
Doug Bentley	Bill Durnan	Dick Irvin	Harry Oliver	Bullet Joe Simpson
Max Bentley	Red Dutton	Busher Jackson	Bert Olmstead	Darryl Sittler
Toe Blake	Babe Dye	Ching Johnson	Bobby Orr	Al Smith
Leo Boivin	Phil Esposito	Moose Johnson	Bernie Parent	Billy Smith
Dickie Boon	Tony Esposito	Tom Johnson	Brad Park	Clint Smith
Mike Bossy	Art Farrell	Aurel Joliat	Lester Patrick	Hooley Smith
Butch Bouchard	Fern Flaman	Duke Keats	Lynn Patrick	Thomas Smith
Buck Boucher	Frank Foyston	Red Kelly	Gilbert Perreault	Allan Stanley
Frank Boucher	Frank Frederickson	Teeder Kennedy	Tommy Phillips	Barney Stanley
John Bower	Bill Gadsby	Dave Keon	Pierre Pilote	Black Jack Stewart
Russell Bowie	Bob Gainey	Elmer Lach	Pit Pitre	Nels Stewart
Frank Brimsek	Chuck Gardiner	Guy Lafleur	Jacques Plante	Bruce Stuart
Punch Broadbent	Herb Gardiner	Newsy Lalonde	Denis Potvin	Hod Stuart
Turk Broda	Jimmy Gardner	Jacques Laperriere	Babe Pratt	Cyclone Taylor
John Bucyk	Bernie Geoffrion	Guy Lapointe	Joe Primeau	Tiny Thompson
Billy Burch	Eddie Gerard	Edgar Laprade	Marcel Pronovost	Vladislav Tretiak
Harry Cameron	Eddie Giacomin	Jack Laviolette	Bob Pulford	Col. Harry Trihey
Gerry Cheevers	Rod Gilbert	Hugh Lehman	Harvey Pulford	Norm Ullman
King Clancy	Billy Gilmour	Jacques Lemaire	Bill Quackenbush	Georges Vezina
Dit Clapper	Moose Goheen	Percy LeSueur	Frank Rankin	Jack Walker
Bobby Clarke	Ebbie Goodfellow	Herb Lewis	Jean Ratelle	Marty Walsh
Sprague Cleghorn	Mike Grant	Ted Lindsay	Chuck Rayner	Harry Watson
Neil Colville	Shorty Green	Harry Lumley	Ken Reardon	Cooney Weiland
Charlie Conacher	Si Griffis	Mickey MacKay	Henri Richard	Harry Westwick
Alex Connell	George Hainsworth	Frank Mahovlich	Maurice Richard	Fred Whitcroft
Bun Cook	Glenn Hall	Joe Malone	George Richardson	Phat Wilson
Art Coulter	Joe Hall	Sylvio Mantha	Gordon Roberts	Gump Worsley
Yvan Cournoyer	Doug Harvey	Jack Marshall	Art Ross	Roy Worters
Bill Cowley	George Hay	Steamer Maxwell	Blair Russel	

ALL-TIME RECORDS

All-Time Goal Leaders

	SEASONS	GAMES	GOALS	GOALS PER GAME
1. Wayne Gretzky	15	1,125	803	.714
2. Gordie Howe	26	1,767	801	.453
3. Marcel Dionne	18	1,348	731	.542
4. Phil Esposito	18	1,282	717	.559
5. Mike Gartner	15	1,170	617	.527
6. Bobby Hull	16	1,063	610	.574
7. Mike Bossy	10	752	573	.762
8. Guy Lafleur	17	1,126	560	.497
9. John Bucyk	23	1,540	556	.361
10. Jari Kurri	13	990	555	.561

All-Time Games Leaders

	SEASONS	GAMES
1. Gordie Howe	26	1,767
2. Alex Delvecchio	24	1,549
3. John Bucyk	23	1,540
4. Tim Horton	24	1,446
5. Harry Howell	21	1,411
6. Norm Ullman	20	1,410
7. Stan Mikita	22	1,394
8. Doug Mohns	22	1,390
9. Larry Robinson	20	1,384
10. Dean Prentice	22	1,378

All-Time Assist Leaders

	SEASONS	GAMES	ASSISTS	ASSISTS PER GAME
1. Wayne Gretzky	15	1,125	1,655	1.471
2. Gordie Howe	26	1,767	1,049	.594
3. Marcel Dionne	18	1,348	1,040	.772
4. Paul Coffey	14	1,033	934	.904
5. Stan Mikita	22	1,394	926	.664
6. Bryan Trottier	18	1,279	901	.704
7. Ray Bourque	15	1,100	877	.797
8. Phil Esposito	18	1,282	873	.681
9. Bobby Clarke	15	1,144	852	.745
10. Mark Messier	15	1,081	838	.775

All-Time Goalie Wins

	WINS	LOSSES	TIES	WIN PERCENTAGE
1. Terry Sawchuk	435	337	188	.551
2. Jacques Plante	434	246	137	.615
3. Tony Esposito	423	307	151	.566
4. Glenn Hall	407	327	165	.544
5. Rogie Vachon	355	291	115	.542
6. Gump Worsley	335	353	150	.489
7. Harry Lumley	332	324	143	.505
8. Billy Smith	305	233	105	.556
9. Andy Moog	303	148	64	.650
10. Turk Broda	302	224	101	.562

All-Time Point Leaders

	SEASONS	GAMES	GOALS	ASSISTS	POINTS	PTS. PER GAME
1. Wayne Gretzky	15	1,125	803	1,655	2,458	2.185
2. Gordie Howe	26	1,767	801	1,049	1,850	1.047
3. Marcel Dionne	18	1,348	731	1,040	1,771	1.314
4. Phil Esposito	18	1,282	717	873	1,590	1.240
5. Stan Mikita	22	1,394	541	926	1,467	1.052
6. Bryan Trottier	18	1,279	524	901	1,425	1.114
7. John Bucyk	23	1,540	556	813	1,369	.889
8. Guy Lafleur	17	1,126	560	793	1,353	1.202
9. Gil Perreault	17	1,191	512	814	1,326	1.113
10. Mark Messier	15	1,081	478	838	1,316	1.217

All-Time Shutout Leaders

	SEASONS	GAMES	SHUTOUTS
1. Terry Sawchuk	21	971	103
2. George Hainsworth	11	464	94
3. Glenn Hall	18	906	84
4. Jacques Plante	18	837	82
5. Alex Connell	12	417	81
6. Tiny Thompson	12	553	81
7. Tony Esposito	18	886	76
8. Lorne Chabot	11	411	73
9. Harry Lumley	16	804	71
10. Roy Worters	12	484	66

All-Time Penalty Leaders				
	Seasons	Games	Pen. Minutes	Pen. Min. Per Game
1. Dave Williams	14	962	3,966	4.12
2. Chris Nilan	13	688	3,043	4.42
3. Dale Hunter	14	1,054	3,005	2.85
4. Tim Hunter	13	675	2,769	4.10
5. Marty McSorley	11	666	2,640	3.96
6. Willie Plett	13	834	2,572	3.08
7. Basil McRae	13	529	2,333	4.41
8. Dave Schultz	9	535	2,294	4.29
9. Laurie Boschman	14	1,009	2,265	2.24
10. Garth Butcher	13	852	2,243	2.63

CLUB ADDRESSES

Boston Bruins
150 Causeway Street
Boston, MA 02114
(617) 227-3206

Buffalo Sabers
Memorial Auditorium
Buffalo, NY 14202
(716) 856-7300

Calgary Flames
Olympic Saddledome
P.O. Box 1540, Station M
Calgary, Alberta T2P 3B9
(403) 261-0475

Chicago Black Hawks
United Center
1901 West Madison Street
Chicago, IL 60612
(312) 455-7000

Dallas Stars
901 Main Street
Suite 2301
Dallas, TX 75202
(214) 712-2890

Detroit Red Wings
Joe Louis Arena
600 Civic Center Drive
Detroit, MI 48226
(313) 396-7544

Edmonton Oilers
7424 118 Avenue
Edmonton, Alberta T5B 4M9
(403) 474-8561

Florida Panthers
100 Northeast Third Avenue
10th Floor
Fort Lauderdale, FL 33301
(305) 768-1900

Hartford Whalers
242 Trumbull Street
8th Floor
Hartford, CT 06103
(203) 728-3366

Los Angeles Kings
Great Western Forum
3900 West Manchester Boulevard
Inglewood, CA 90305
(310) 419-3160

Mighty Ducks of Anaheim
Arrowhead Pond
2695 Katella Avenue
Anaheim, CA 92803-6177
(714) 704-2700

Montreal Canadiens
Montreal Forum
2313 St. Catherine Street West
Montreal, Quebec H3H 1N2
(514) 932-2582

New Jersey Devils
Meadowlands Arena
P.O. Box 504
East Rutherford, NJ 07073
(201) 935-6050

New York Islanders
Nassau Coliseum
Uniondale, NY 11553
(516) 794-4100

New York Rangers
Madison Square Garden
4 Pennsylvania Plaza
New York, NY 10001
(212) 465-6000

Ottawa Senators
301 Moodie Drive
Suite 200
Nepean, Ontario K2H 9C4
(613) 721-0115

Philadelphia Flyers
The Spectrum
3601 South Broad Street
Philadelphia, PA 19148
(215) 465-4500

Pittsburgh Penguins
Civic Arena
Pittsburgh, PA 15219
(412) 642-1800

Quebec Nordiques
Colisee de Quebec
2205 Avenue du Colisee
Quebec City, Quebec G1L 4W7
(418) 529-8441

St. Louis Blues
Kiel Center
1401 Clark Avenue
St. Louis, MO 63103
(314) 622-2500

San Jose Sharks
San Jose Arena
525 West Santa Clara Street
San Jose, CA 95113
(408) 287-7070

Tampa Bay Lightning
501 East Kennedy Boulevard
Suite 175
Tampa, FL 33602
(813) 229-2658

Toronto Maple Leafs
Maple Leaf Gardens
60 Carlton Street
Toronto, Ontario M5B 1L1
(416) 977-1641

Vancouver Canucks
Pacific Coliseum
100 North Renfrew Street
Vancouver, British Columbia V5K 3N7
(604) 254-5141

Washington Capitals
US Air Arena
1 Harry S. Truman Drive
Landover, MD 20785
(301) 386-7000

Winnipeg Jets
Winnipeg Arena
15-1430 Maroons Road
Winnipeg, Manitoba R3G 0L5
(204) 982-5387

Hockey Hall of Fame
BCE Place
30 Yonge Street
Toronto, Ontario M5E 1X8
(416) 360-7735

PHOTOGRAPHY CREDITS

ALLSPORT: ©Allsport USA: 8, 29 (left),
32 (both), 104, 105
©Harry Scull/Allsport: 11, 17, 29
(right)
©C.J. Relke/Allsport: 28
©Robert Laberge/Allsport: 47, 51
©Al Bello/Allsport: 97 (right)

AP/WIDE WORLD PHOTOS: 3, 10, 14,
16 (right), 31, 35, 44, 64, 73, 78, 82,
85, 86, 87, 98 (left), 103, 110 (right)

BRUCE BENNETT STUDIOS: 6, 25, 27
(right)
©M. DiGiacomo/BBS: 12, 13 (top),
21 (top), 22 (left), 26, 40, 56,
89, 109
©J. Giamundo/BBS: 18, 49 (right)
©Scott Levy/BBS: 19
©Bruce Bennett/BBS: 21 (bottom),
22 (right), 30 (left), 37, 39, 42, 43,
45, 46, 48, 49, 53 (left), 57 (background), 59, 94, 95, 96, 97 (top center), 98 (right), 107 (right), 108
©J. DiMaggio/J. Kalish/BBS: 24
©A. Foxall/BBS: 97 (top left)

BETTMANN NEWSPHOTOS: 90, 91,
92, 101, 102, 106, 107 (left)

HOCKEY HALL OF FAME: ©Frank
Prazak/HHOF: 2, 9, 13 (bottom
right), 36, 67 (background) 100,
110 (left), 111
©Hockey Hall of Fame: 23, 33, 34,
54, 55, 61 (both), 63, 65, 70-71, 72,
75, 76, 79, 80
©Graphics Artists/HHOF: 27, 88
©Doug MacLellan/HHOF: 50
©Imperial Oil Turofaky/HHOF: 77

UPI/BETTMANN: 13 (bottom left), 16
(left), 20, 41, 57 (inset), 60, 62, 84

INDEX